Business *to* Brand

For Dad, who forever told me the world is full of good people trying to do good things.

Much of the planning and writing of this book was completed in my home office in North Warrandyte, Australia. I would like to acknowledge the traditional owners and custodians of this land, the Woi-Wurrung and Wurundjeri people of the Kulin Nation and pay my respects to their elders, past and present. As a small business owner working and living on these lands I pledge to work in ways that aid in bringing equality and equity to First Nations peoples.

Business
to Brand

**Moving from
transaction to
transformation**

Fiona Killackey

Hardie Grant

BOOKS

Contents

Introduction

Think back to the last thing you bought that made you feel really good.

It might have been a product you have always wanted to own, or perhaps it was a service you had been looking forward to engaging with and it exceeded your expectations.

Chances are, this positive impact on your psyche, and even your life, came about as a result of you feeling an emotional connection to whatever it was you bought; an alignment between your values and beliefs and the brand you were connecting with.

Now, consider the business you're currently running.

What percentage of your audience would say they feel that same alignment or joy when they buy from you? What about when they simply interact with you via any one of the number of marketing channels you may be utilising? How many people would look at your business and, despite all competition, consider it to be their number one choice? How many of your customers and clients would look at what you have created not simply as a business, but as a brand?

Anyone can start a business.

In Australia alone, forty new companies are founded every single hour and there are, as of 2023, almost 2.6 million active businesses. Across the globe in the US, there are 33.2 million of them (as of 2023) and in the UK it's a substantial 5.6 million. In India, it is estimated that as of 2023 there are between 43 and 50 million businesses (however a much smaller percentage have been formally registered as companies) and in China, for the same year, it's approximately 52.8 million.

But for all these businesses – millions of which started perhaps with money and time dedicated to visual branding (a logo, colour palette and social media icons) – how many actually took the time to create and cultivate a brand?

What does it really take to transition from a business to a brand?

What does it take to create an entity that truly aligns with its values (both externally and internally)?

How can you inject the humanity so deeply desired by present and future generations into a business now so that it becomes a trusted brand tomorrow?

How do you cultivate a culture within your company so that your staff and suppliers become your best brand ambassadors?

How do you create a roadmap that futureproofs your strategy and overall direction?

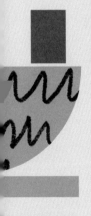

How can you build a brand, not just a business?

This is one of the key questions I help my clients answer and, within the pages of this book, I will help you to do the same.

It's important to acknowledge up-front that the word 'brand' may be polarising to some people reading this. Perhaps you prefer the word 'company' or 'entity'. Perhaps you feel sickened by the idea that everyone and anything is a brand, and shy away from alignment to that word. Perhaps you believe that the word 'brand' is only ever to be used for giant multinational corporations that are inherently greedy, ruining the planet and after only one thing: profit.

I would urge you to consider another way of thinking about the word 'brand' as you read this book, especially in relation to your own business.

When I talk about 'brand' in this book, I'm referring to an entity that has meaning, purpose and a positive impact on its audience/s and on the world at large. It is about creating a company that has, at its essence, a reason for people to believe in what it offers – not just in the way of products and services, but in its approach to people and to the planet.

So many of us want to create a business that helps people and the planet, that fills a gap in people's lives and becomes a trusted, go-to source for whatever it is they need or desire. If you started your business with the hope that it would not only bring you financial fulfilment, but also emotional contentment, then building a brand is an essential part of the process.

Through frameworks, interviews and proven strategies, this book will provide you with the practical steps to help transform your business into an entity that you can be proud of. Along the way it will help guide you through questions about your hopes for the world, the legacy you wish to leave and the way you'll run your business on a day-to-day level.

Whether you are just starting out or decades into your business journey, you will learn the essential ingredients for moving your audience from simply transacting with your business to being *transformed* by your brand.

Business *to* Brand

How to use this book

This book is broken into twelve key chapters, each of which relates to an area of moving from business to brand. While you can read any chapter at any time, the concepts and ideas build on one another, compounding and deepening your understanding as you go. It's for this reason that I suggest you read and work through the book (making any notes as you go – yes, it's okay to write in a book, I encourage it!) from start to finish. Once you have read it completely, feel free to go back as and when you need to, utilising this as a reference book for your brand journey. It's my hope that this will become your go-to guide for building, analysing and revising your brand now and well into the future.

Within each chapter you will find suggested tasks to consider and work through (these will be shown with a ✒ next to them). Depending on where you are in your own business and brand journey, some of these may take minutes, while others may take a much longer time, hours or maybe even days. If you are new to these concepts, please be kind to yourself. The last thing I'd want is for this book to add any more pressure than what already exists for anyone running a small business and building a brand. Remember, building a brand is not something you do once, but rather – like being in a relationship – it is a choice you make every single day.

At the end of each chapter you will also find activities or questions to consider (these will be shown with a ☰ next to them). These are there to pique your curiosity and help you think more critically about how you transform your business to a brand. Utilise these as and when they feel right.

Throughout this book, you will find templates, frameworks and diagrams that provide practical tools for establishing a strong brand. You will find digital copies for some of these, free for you to download, at **mydailybusiness.com/brandbook**. Wherever you see this icon ⬇ you will know you can simply visit the URL above, or for ease you can also scan the QR code below.

Nestled among the main chapters are interviews with people leading successful brands. I have chosen a mix of businesses, from global names that have been around for decades, through to newer brands that you may not have heard of just yet. Each of the people interviewed has embraced the idea of building a brand (or, in Vitsœ's case, a company), not just a business and, in turn, has enabled their audiences to become advocates and ambassadors, moving them from simply transacting to being transformed.

 Scan to access
digital downloads

Your journey from business to brand

Each person's journey in building a brand is unique. What works for someone else may not feel in alignment for you. What you want from the brand you are building, and what your audience desires, will be different from other brands and it's important to remember this as you move along in this journey.

In this book you will find templates and frameworks that ask you to look inwards; that help you to come up with a strategy and way forward that best aligns with your values and beliefs, and that genuinely represents how you want your brand to have an impact – on you, on your audience and on the world.

I've built my own business and brand, My Daily Business, and worked with large brands (think Amazon, Etsy, L'Oréal and Audible) through to more than 1000 smaller brands (from Collective Closets and Cargo Crew to Mustard and Mutual Muse), so I know that these frameworks work, no matter the size or sector of business.

Before you dive into this book, take some time to journal or meditate, or just get still and consider what a 'brand' really means to you. If you have any hesitations about the term 'brand', consider where these are coming from and the drivers behind these feelings.

Then, in a quiet and calm space, consider:

- What legacy do you want to leave with your brand?
- Who does your brand best serve?
- What are the values and beliefs that underpin your brand?
- How does your brand differ from other brands in the market?
- What do you hope people say about your brand when you're not around?
- How will your brand positively change the world?

These may seem like BIG questions, but the best brands really do impact the world. What impact will yours have?

Building a brand can be an adventure, one filled with interesting discoveries, one that changes and adapts when it needs to, and one that is overall an incubator for human connection. The tactics and frameworks in this book may be new to you, or there may be some you have already encountered. I urge you to take on the challenges and tasks in this book with the open mind of an adventurer, getting curious about what it is you're learning and how you'll relay these discoveries to those who choose to connect with your small business as it makes its way to becoming a brand.

Lastly, remember that this is your own journey and that, in many ways, creating a brand is a mysterious process. What works for you may not work for someone else who has a very similar business and way of working, or vice versa. And while these frameworks and steps will help you gain more clarity, direction and alignment in everything that you are creating, building a brand and evolving it takes time and an open mind. It also takes a willingness to embrace – and enjoy – the journey without always knowing exactly where it will lead you.

Consider the words of Albert Einstein, who said: 'The most beautiful experience we can have is the mysterious. It is the fundamental emotion that stands at the cradle of true art and true science.'

I wish you all the best as you embark on this adventure.

Fiona

'Building a brand and evolving it takes time and an open mind. It also takes a willingness to embrace – and enjoy – the journey without always knowing exactly where it will lead you.'

Business *to* Brand

01.

How did we get here?

In July 2001, just three days after turning twenty-one, I found myself cashing in a one-way ticket from Melbourne to London. I had saved the $800 required for the flight from a part-time cafe job and organised my first month's rental with a stranger I had met online. I had a Bachelor of Arts, and to me that equalled guaranteed employment. I envisioned myself working in London at the top magazines of the time – *Dazed & Confused*, *i-D* and *NME*. I imagined a life of abundance; European holidays on rotation, magnificent cutting-edge fashion and a flash East End apartment to call home.

The reality was a little less exciting.

The rental I had organised came complete with a strange American flatmate, who would only open his bedroom door a tiny crack to talk to me, so that for the entire month I lived there I never actually saw his whole face. After interviewing at a bunch of magazines, I was offered a stint working three days a week at one of the women's glossies – for the grand total of £0. After spending the first week dusting a makeup closet, and the second week calling PR agents to find out what dress a celebrity had been wearing, I decided the fairytale I had written for myself might well need to be edited. My decision to leave came four weeks later when I noticed one of my colleagues wheeling a suitcase around the office. Excited, I asked if she was finally going on a photoshoot. She replied no and informed me that she was technically homeless and would often sleep at work or stay at a friend's house. As such, she carted her belongings everywhere she went. My colleague had been working full-time for two years for free.

In the months that followed, I left the magazine industry and, following a disastrous period of au-pairing for a wealthy family across from Hampstead Heath, I finally landed a job as the executive assistant to the managing director at a small Shadwell advertising agency. I moved into a share house in Bethnal Green with two wonderful flatmates. It was above a workman's cafe that opened at 5 am and served a full fry-up breakfast for three quid and a coffee for just 50p (prices I would come to love as my savings dwindled). Next door to that and directly below my room was a makeshift cab station where drivers would congregate from dusk till dawn, laughing, smoking and generally making it impossible to sleep.

For a full 40-hour work week I was paid just over £200 (before tax). The majority of this went towards rent and public transport, with a small amount left over for socialising, internet cafes (remember those?) and food. Despite the super-tight purse strings, the one thing I was happy to spend my money on was tea. In particular, a herbal tea by a certain brand I had grown accustomed to having once or twice a week prior to leaving Australia. When I had used up the tea I had brought with me, I tried to find a similar one in London's supermarkets. Given London is a global city and the capital of a country renowned for its love affair with tea, I thought the task would be relatively straightforward. Like my stint in UK magazines, however, it turned out to be a lot harder than I had expected.

Even after trekking to all parts of the city, including specialty tea shops, I couldn't locate a tea that had the same taste as the one I enjoyed back home. In the end, I asked my mum to send packets of this particular tea from Australia. Despite taking up to a month to arrive, the wait was worth it; I'd light up every time a new parcel arrived. For much of that time living in London I would get into work early to utilise the free bread and butter in the office kitchen so I could eat something substantial during the day, and in the evenings I took to buying the cheapest

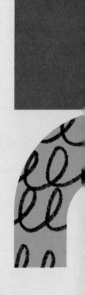

How did we get here?

of cheap cans of spaghetti from Tesco and happily agreed to any leftovers that my flatmates – both amazing cooks – offered up. But when I had a cup of that tea, it felt somehow indulgent, as if I wasn't living pay cheque to pay cheque. It sounds ridiculous but that tea gave me a sense that things would get better; that despite the challenges around me, there would always be those calming moments with a quality cup of tea.

More than twenty years on, I still occasionally indulge and buy that same tea. And just as I have grown and changed, so too has the brand. While in my early twenties I was attracted to it mainly for its taste, today I continue to engage with it because of the brand's approach to sustainability. My income and living situation may have changed, but the connection I have with that brand hasn't.

We all have them: brands we stay loyal to; brands we admire, respect and count among the things we find it hard to live without; brands we have continued to buy from, recommend and respect for years, if not decades.

Perhaps they are the brands our parents or grandparents brought into the home and therefore feel a little nostalgic to us. Or perhaps they are the brands we were able to save for and finally buy with our first pay cheques. Maybe they are brands you dreamt of owning as a child and now, as an adult, they give you a sense of joy every time you engage with them. Perhaps they are brands you have only found out about more recently and have connected with on an emotional level. Maybe they are brands that give you hope about the future, or maybe they are brands that always make you smile despite life's tougher moments.

These brands have made their way into our lives and, much like my own experience with tea, we can easily relay to friends, colleagues and family a story about our unique relationship with them.

On the flip side, there are hundreds of products and services we will use in our lifetime where we fail to develop a relationship with or connection to the business behind it.

We may buy these products simply because they are the cheapest, or the most convenient, or because we were served up an ad on social media in the midst of midnight scrolling and it seemed like a good idea at the time. Most likely, we will not relay their story to anyone or share in their celebrations. We will not bother to follow them on social accounts or subscribe to their emails. We will not willingly choose to form any sort of connection. We will simply use (or dispose of) their product or service then forget they ever existed. And when we have a need (or a want) for a similar product or service in the future, we will not type their business name into a search engine because we have simply forgotten about them.

They are nameless and faceless. We don't know the humans working for them and, in many cases, we forget there are even people involved between the idea and delivery of the product or service. They are not the brands we use to help us show our values, beliefs and hopes to the world. They are not the brands we scan for first at the supermarket or see the colours and logos of on the shelves of our homes and workplaces month after month, year after year. They are not the brands whose stories we share with friends and family who visit and ask where that sofa or ceramic cup is from. These nameless and faceless entities may fill a practical need for a fleeting moment in time, but they are ultimately forgettable.

Business *to* Brand

You may be wondering why building a brand should even matter if we are already using these nameless and faceless businesses? Why should anyone want to move from running a small business to being the founder of a brand? In an age where you can literally find any product or service in seconds and filter by the cheapest possible option, what importance does *brand* actually play?

The answer is a considerable one.

It's for exactly this reason – the competition and overabundance of options – that creating a brand has never been as important.

We live in a time unlike any other that has come before it. Where once you had to commute to a physical location to buy something – perhaps your local butcher to buy meat or your local seamstress to buy a new dress – today you can buy anything you want, need or suddenly desire within seconds. The arrival of eCommerce and companies like Amazon, ASOS and Adore Beauty has changed what shopping looks like, with millions of products able to be bought by anyone with a wi-fi connection. Similarly, service-based business platforms like Fiverr, Upwork and Airtasker have massively reduced the time it takes to find a contractor and, in some cases, the price that contractor will charge.

In today's world, it is virtually impossible to cut through the noise and beat our competition solely on rational factors like price or proximity. No matter what you are offering, there will always be another business or entity ready to undercut you on price or delivery time (or both). With literally thousands of different marketing channels, companies can target your audience like never before and offer them something cheaper, quicker and in more colour options. Perhaps that undercutter may even be you if your sole purpose for being in business is financial gain. If so, it goes without saying that in time the constant pace and need to keep up with competitors and newcomers in the market may lead to burnout, exhaustion and financial challenges. There are very few small businesses who can survive competition for years on end with multinational giants by cutting their margins and overheads.

If instead you started your business to have a greater impact on those around you, as well as cultivate financial freedom and control over your time, reduce harm to the planet and/or give back in some way, then your products and/or services need to be seen as something worth paying more for, or taking the additional effort to seek out.

So how do you garner attention for your business when virtually every market is saturated and millions of people are starting new businesses every single day?

By building a *brand*, not just a *business*.

When you create a brand, you are creating a vision that attracts and encourages people to be a part of it. You are bringing people together who align with the values and beliefs that act as the foundation for your brand. In essence, you are creating a community that not only understands why you do what you do as a business, but also understands how their connection with it helps the world at large.

When people believe in and feel connected to a brand they are more likely to relay stories about it to others, share it on social media and recommend it to friends and family. This not only has an impact on your greater vision (i.e. the

How did we get here?

purpose you have for the business, which is now shared amongst your audiences) but also on your bottom line.

Financially, building a brand enables you to attract people who feel attuned to your values, mission and vision and who may well become long-term brand-loyal customers. It's thought to cost up to ten times more (in terms of ad spend and brand marketing) to gain a new customer than to get someone who has already experienced your brand to purchase again. By building a brand, you are inviting people to stay connected with you (e.g. through social channels or a regular email newsletter), and in doing so, you are increasing the chance that they will connect again with your brand (e.g. by purchasing or sharing your communications with someone else who may then go on to purchase).

If the brand you are building is genuinely seeking to invest in a more positive global future, you may be looking at creating more ethical supply chains, implementing a robust recycling and waste management policy, and giving back to the community in various ways. You are also likely to be a welcome place for people from all walks of life, a brand that celebrates diversity and encourages inclusion, and a safe and trusted source from which to invest in products and services.

These are all factors that can encourage brand loyalty, enable greater awareness through word of mouth and referral marketing, and become the reason someone chooses your product, experience or service over a competitor.

In fact, the Global Sustainability Study 2021 conducted by Simon-Kucher & Partners (a global strategy and pricing consultancy) found that 85% of people have shifted their purchase behaviour towards being more sustainable in the past five years.

That is a huge number of potential customers who will be seeking out ethical brands that they can form a long-lasting relationship with. This is also good for business in a financial sense, with return or repeat customers being one of the key metrics for strong financial performance.

Building a brand also allows you to attract quality staff who are excited about your vision and aligned with your brand values, and who feel they are contributing to the overall mission and success of the business.

In research carried out by Global Tolerance, wherein more than 2000 people in the UK were questioned, 44% thought meaningful work that helped others was more important than what they would be paid and 36% said they would work harder in their roles if they felt the brand or company they were working for benefited society.

If you're reading this and are lucky enough to have staff, you'll know how hard it can be to find great people, and how much time and financial resources are poured into hiring (and sometimes firing) staff. It's in your best interest, financial and otherwise, to hire and retain people who will feel called to show up and are invested in their work.

Outside of financial reasons, there are also the emotional benefits of building a brand. If, like me, you started a business not purely as a way to make an income, but to do something meaningful with your life and to have a positive impact on the world, then a brand will help you do that.

By creating a brand you have the opportunity to change the narrative around current world challenges by utilising the community your brand attracts to better the world around you. Perhaps you'll use your brand authority to champion environmental work and fight climate change, perhaps you'll use it to stand up for the rights of minority groups and fight racism or ableism, or maybe you'll utilise it to bring awareness to domestic violence, ageism or mental health. Whatever the cause, you can actively work to have an impact when you build a brand that encourages people not only to transact with a product, experience or service, but also to be transformed by everything that the brand champions.

Lastly, building a brand enables you, the founder, to gain greater fulfilment from life. This might seem like an outlandish, or even selfish, statement, but if you consider how many hours, days, weeks, months and years you will spend advocating for your business, you want all of that time to mean something. Most people have a hope of leaving some sort of legacy, some recognition that their time on earth held purpose or meaning. By building a brand, particularly one that is genuinely aligned with its values and beliefs and able to create real connections with its audiences, you are fuelling that legacy and personal fulfilment.

So how do you even start? Where do you begin?

In the following chapters, we will walk through what 'brand' actually means, and the various steps you'll need to take to build or cement yours, as well as how to change and adapt when necessary. We will discuss everything from setting up your brand foundations and diving into the purpose and impact behind your ideas, through to the way you'll express the brand in your communications, channel selection and positioning, as well as strategically mapping out your brand elevation and cultivating your brand authority. We will look at where you are today and your goals for tomorrow, who else you will need to bring into the mix and the day-to-day activities that will keep your brand focused and committed to your overall vision.

So many small business owners I meet talk about brand or branding as if it is purely choosing a colour palette, typography or logo. It's my hope that by working through this book and completing the tasks as you go, you'll realise just how much more a brand really is, and what a powerful impact it can have on you, your community and the world at large.

How did we get here?

TASKS TO CONSIDER

Before we jump into Chapter 2 and define what a brand actually is, it's worthwhile taking some time to reflect on what you have just read.

Work through the following questions or download them in a worksheet form online via the QR code below.

1.   *When you think of the term 'brand', what comes to mind?*

2.   *Where do these thoughts derive from? Are they negative or positive?*

3.   *Which brands do you personally have an affinity with?*

4.   *What is it about them that you like?*

5.   *Likewise, which brands turn you off?*

6.   *What is it about them you don't like?*

7.   *Which causes are you passionate about?*

8.   *How can you link these causes to what your business offers?*

Once you have your answers, it's time to jump into Chapter 2.

Scan for digital
worksheet

02.

What is a brand?

What comes to mind when you think of the term 'brand'?

Does it bring up negative imagery of greedy multinational corporations, sucking the earth's resources dry? Or social media influencers spruiking their courses on 'creating your personal brand'? Perhaps it makes you think of giant logos atop huge trucks shipping products along bustling highways. Or stamps and hot irons branding cattle.

Or perhaps, as with many people, the term conjures up images of logos, typography pairings and colour palettes. After all, this is what most people have grown up to believe. Coca-Cola = red and white. Pepsi = black and blue. It makes sense then that when it comes to starting or scaling their own small business, most people will think that 'building a brand' is simply making a choice between a fat typeface or a skinny script, pastel or neon colours, or a .com suffix vs a more creative one.

In reality, the visual communication element is simply one of the finishing touches of a brand, akin to the buttons sewn onto a jacket. Well before that button is sewn on, that jacket will have gone through numerous stages from initial design concepts through to final sketch, then onto patterns being cut, samples being made, tweaked then made again, fabric being sought and checked against ethical supply chain metrics, fabric being rolled out and measured, layers being put together and adjusted numerous times, threads selected, finishes and trimmings chosen until … at last, the buttons can be sewn on.

Likewise, a brand needs to travel through many points before a visual identity can be layered onto it. From brand ideation and bigger-picture thinking (vision, values, mission) through to competitor analysis, communication strategy and channel selection, the elements of a brand are so much greater than what the logo looks like or which colour palette will be utilised for the website.

If this is the case, then why is there such a strong link between the idea of a 'brand' and the image of a logo? To answer this, we need to look at where the idea of a 'brand' began.

The idea of differentiating our wares, livestock and creations from others via some sort of visual signal is nothing new. The first forms of branding – that is, actually burning a symbol into something such as a box or (unfortunately for them) an animal – were shown to have taken place thousands of years ago. In fact, the very word 'brand' derives from the Old Norse word *brandr*, which means 'to burn', and it was common for farmers through to traders to burn symbols onto things to show and mark ownership.

From as early as 2700 BCE, Ancient Egyptians were shown to have branded their cattle, using symbols and shapes that relayed one person's or family's ownership of animals over another. In Ancient Pompeii bakers would brand their bread either with stamps that spelled out the maker and area, or with the baker's own thumbprints. In Andrew Wallace-Hadrill's book *Herculaneum: Past and Future*, he describes the incredible find of archaeologists who uncovered a fully intact carbonised loaf of bread dating all the way back to the early years of the common era. The bread, baked and cut in the shape of 'Panis Quadratus' (i.e. a round loaf cut into eight equal parts like a pizza), also showed a stamp with the maker's mark on it. The reason for doing this was believed to be so that those eating the bread knew who made it. This discovery is fascinating, especially when we consider how

What is a brand?

'modern' we may find being able to track, through QR codes for example, where items have come from and who made them.

Later, across to the East in China, the use of blocks and the first example of paper (believed to have been invented by a Chinese court official around 105 CE) would come to allow traders to showcase their wares and describe their items to the masses via symbols and markings. This time in history (think just prior to the *Game of Thrones* era if you need a visual) marks the beginning of what we now know as advertising, with the inventions in China giving traders and those in power the ability to create printed banners, wrapping, market collateral and tangible items that enabled people to distinguish one 'brand' from another.

By the 1500s most farming cultures had some way of 'branding' their cattle and using these symbols to denote their location, quality and even ways of farming. It was individual and instantly recognisable within local communities. And it was not until a century or so later that branding began to move from being something that was done individually by people within a community into something that could be done en masse with the introduction of mass manufacturing.

Known as the Industrial Age, the 1700s and 1800s changed the way products and produce were created. Add to this the fact that trade was happening on a grander scale and more items were moving around the world, and you had a need arising for differentiation or a way of standing out (similar to what the internet has done for businesses now). When a local company, farm or trader was only selling within their own community, people could recognise a stamp or brand and understand the item's or animal's origins. This became harder to do as competition swept in.

Enter: The Trademark. This was a way to legally identify who a mark, symbol, series of words, shapes or colours belonged to, with legal ramifications for those attempting to impersonate it.

Now, remember the bread they found all the way back from 1 CE? Well, it's not just the bread that came full circle – haha! #TotalDadJoke – we are coming full circle now as the idea of the trademark was actually first put into place in the UK around 1266, while the empire was under the reign of Henry III, in relation to bakeries and breadmakers. Despite Henry's best efforts (and those of Belgian and German beer houses like Stella Artois and Löwenbräu whose trademarks are said to have begun in the 1300s), it would take a few hundred more years before the idea of a trademark became 'official-official' in the wider world.

In the US in the late 1700s, sailcloth manufacturers petitioned Thomas Jefferson (who was then a secretary of state but who would become the third president of the US shortly thereafter) on the need for a law to help trademark their wares nationally. He agreed and began to get things in place – but not before the French, who passed the first full comprehensive trademark system in the world in 1857. Not wanting to be left behind, the US – who had been caught up in the usual political red tape that seems to hinder most good ideas – entered treaties for reciprocal protection of trademarks with Russia, Belgium and France. The laws they enacted got a bit of backlash and, despite creating the *1881 Trademark Act*, people didn't come forward in decent numbers to register trademarks (around 4000 a year) until 1905 (the time it took to get the original 1881 Act to a position that was useful to traders). This became known as the 1905 Act.

You have to remember, this was a time of mass change for the world, with railway systems enabling greater travel for both people and products and the ability for 'brands' to be seen, loved and desired globally. Not only did this lead to a greater need for the trademark industry, but also for the protection of patents, inventions and business designs, which paved the way for the 1883 Paris Convention. According to the World Intellectual Property Organization, the convention 'applies to industrial property in the widest sense, including patents, trademarks, industrial designers, utility models, service marks, trade names, geographical indications and the repression of unfair competition'.

But does a brand just equate to having a trademark?

No.

So, when did the brand evolve to what we know it as today?

One of the most popular TV series in the last decade has been *Mad Men*, a show centred around the characters of a prestigious New York advertising agency in the early 1960s. It's in this era that the next important marker in brand history is set.

The 1950s through to the 1980s are known as the 'golden era' of advertising. This was when many people in the West had access to more media – from magazines and newspapers, through to radio and television. It was also when companies were able to directly message their audiences through advertisements in these mediums on a scale that hadn't been seen before. Companies began to get inside the minds of their audiences to figure out how their audiences desired to be seen, and subsequently how they could get their brand to be a part of that vision.

Those 'mad men' (a colloquial term for those working in advertising on Madison Avenue, New York, in the 1950s) were in charge of bringing these companies to life and shaping perception. For example, Marlboro, a cigarette company launched in the 1920s which had previously aimed its product at women (with campaigns including 'Mommy's Marlboros' in the 1950s), began shifting the brand's perception with the help of Leo Burnett (a 'mad man'), and by the 1960s had reinvented itself as a masculine man's choice, reflective of the popularity of Western films and their leading men. If you're a 'real man', you'll smoke Marlboro.

By the late 1970s and into the 1980s, marketing and the idea of selling your brand story became a more important element of company structures, with businesses competing across multiple touchpoints for the most creative and innovative way to get their messages across. It was around the same time that *AdNews* magazine and *Marketing Week* – both publications still utilised by marketing professionals today – launched.

The 1990s changed things again with the arrival of 'the internet' into the mainstream. By this time many people in the West were beginning to invest in a home computer and, in the second half of the '90s, they went 'online'. In 1993 just over 100 websites existed, but by 1997 it was estimated that there were as many as 100,000 websites. One of those websites was Amazon.com which launched in 1996, and by the end of the decade (according to an article in *Publishers Weekly* from July 2000) it boasted more than 16.9 million users, with sales increasing from $610 million in 1998 to $1.64 billion the following year (a 169% increase). Amazon's arrival forever changed the way people would shop and experience brands in this new age and heralded the start of eCommerce as we know it today.

What is a brand?

A handful of years later in 2004, Harvard student Mark Zuckerberg (along with roommates Eduardo Saverin, Andrew McCollum, Dustin Moskovitz and Chris Hughes) created what would become Facebook, an online platform that initially began as a way to stay in touch with friends and family, and which has grown (alongside other companies within the Meta empire like Instagram and WhatsApp) to become one of the leading marketing platforms for businesses. Unlike anything that has come before, social media has enabled companies to build their brand profile, connect with audiences in new ways and extensively understand the competitor landscape. It has also changed the way audiences can research, interrogate, scrutinise, connect with and better understand their favourite brands.

So, with all of this history front of mind – from the branding of cattle through to brand marketing across social media – what exactly is a *brand*?

Your brand is what you create (product, company, business) in addition to the recognised perception in your audience's mind around those creations. Your brand is your promise to your audience and the way in which you uphold it. It is the gut feeling and expectation that your brand evokes for those engaging with it and the attributes that fuel those feelings. Your brand is brought to life through your vision, values, voice and visuals. Your brand is that essence – often mysterious and hard to perfectly articulate – that differentiates you from your competitors and enables those engaging with it to see it as much more than a business.

Because today it's not just your trademark that needs to stand out (and believe me, anyone who has tried to take another entity or individual to court to prove their trademark knows it can feel virtually impossible to enact), it's your entire brand makeup.

Every single part of your brand can be dissected, analysed and reviewed – and it will be.

A brand today has to be consistent in every single touchpoint, from the tone of the person who answers your customer service questions, to the length of time it takes your website to load, through to the choice of handwash in your bathrooms. Do all of these things represent what your brand stands for? Does it represent your brand's personality? Does it align with the brand's core values? Does it help guide people from the stage of research to one of evaluation and eventually advocacy?

A brand is as complex, considered, curious and culpable as any one person on earth – perhaps more so as it will often have far more followers, subscribers, users and customers than any one of us has close friends. And every single one of those customers needs to feel valued, appreciated and taken care of in every step of their buyer journey (even the ones who never buy). In fact, it's this change – the consumer or audience deciding how you fare – that is one of the most important aspects to keep in mind when considering what a 'brand' means today. So much of how a brand is seen in the wider world not only comes down to the messages being put out into the market by the business, but also – perhaps, *more* so – the messages being put out about the company by its customers, followers and audience. Today, buying into or supporting a brand is a way of expressing what we believe in ourselves, which communities we wish to be a part of and what we prioritise. We express what is important to us through the choices we make when we buy; the brands we allow into our homes, workplaces and lives.

Business *to* Brand

For example, consider the supermarket you most frequently shop at. It may simply be the store closest to you, in which case shopping there is convenient and saves you time that you can spend doing other things you deem more important. Others may travel to a specialty supermarket that stocks the brands they enjoy cooking with. Others may look for a supermarket that stocks the freshest ingredients or those less harmful to the planet. And others may opt for a discount supermarket where the brand is less important than the price. (Of course, for many people, the last option is a necessity rather than a choice.)

Years ago I lived in London (remember my indulgent tea choices?) and would often change supermarkets depending on who I was preparing food for. For me and my husband, the local Tesco or Turkish corner store sufficed. But if we were having relatives over, I might have branched out to Sainsbury's or, if I really wanted to impress, Waitrose.

While most supermarkets will sell the same items (e.g. milk, bread, eggs), they will also have spent considerable time and money on marketing their brands in ways that will attract their ideal audiences (and in doing so, possibly repel others). If the number one message is 'shop here to save money', this will be reflected in the supermarket's advertising and brand communications. Likewise, if the main message is 'shop here if you want quality', the advertising and marketing collateral will mirror this. If a brand is seeking to increase its audience or sales in a particular period, it may borrow a main message from another brand temporarily. For example, while we rarely bought food from M&S (Marks & Spencer), we would shop there when it ran its 'two for a tenner' campaigns, which enabled us to buy a full three-course meal and bottle of wine for just £10. In this way, M&S was attracting the clientele who might usually shop elsewhere (read: Tesco) and hoping that a positive customer experience might lead to it being considered as an option the next time we needed food.

A brand today must be absolutely clear on its vision – what it is trying to achieve in the long term – as well as who it is for. It must understand and authentically align with its values – the guiding principles that impact its offerings and its marketing and connection channels as well as the visuals, personality, positioning and voice that will bring all of that to life. To build a brand today is to consider all of those elements that make for an emotional connection between audience and business.

We will dive into each of these elements in more detail within this book, but for now let's get an understanding of how much more is involved in the making of a brand outside of its visual components.

The idea of a brand can be divided into three areas and for ease of remembering I've created an acronym: ACE.

ACE

If you consider the meaning of the word 'ace', which is a noun, adjective and a verb, it can describe:

- high marks (e.g. she *aced* her test)

- exceptional skills (e.g. she was *ace* at basketball, or he is a riding *ace*)

- a shot within the game of tennis that is usually so strong that the opponent cannot return it

- a playing card which is usually ranked as the highest card in most suits (the *ace* of spades).

In terms of brand, I believe an ACE brand can:

- consistently hit high marks (for the range of metrics it deems important) in the minds of its audiences – past, present and potential

- show exceptional skills in the way it delivers its products, experiences and services

- present experiences and a community that are so good they make alternative brands obsolete

- become the number one (and possibly only good) choice in its industry or sector.

So what does ACE stand for?

- **A = Authenticity** Any meaningful brand needs to lead with authenticity and boast a strong foundation to build upon. A strong brand is one that is solid, grounded in purpose and secure enough to withstand the inevitable changes and influences that will impact any brand as it grows. Ironically, the word authenticity has been so overused in recent times that you may immediately feel inauthentic using it. If this is the case, I would ask you to consider the original meaning of the word, which comes from the Greek *authentikos*, meaning original, genuine and principal. It is only from an authentic starting point that brands can elicit genuine transformation in their audiences.

- **C = Creativity** A strong brand is one in which its creativity – from its positioning through to its personality – aids in shaping perception and enabling its audience to know it is the most desired choice for them. It is about bringing the brand foundations to life through the use of visuals and voice, and enabling its audiences to feel an emotional connection with its content, messaging, name and story. A solid brand also remembers that its audience is made up of real people, individuals who buy into this brand and create communities around it. Good brands feed a need or desire within an individual to think: *yes, this is the one for me.*

- **E = Elevation** A great brand is conscious of its elevation. This is not necessarily just financial growth or physical expansion, but understanding the need to adapt to its audience's desires, as well as the internal and external factors which require it to level up. Just like humans, a brand needs to grow and develop to keep living, becoming stronger and more meaningful over time. Its elevation may well show up in financial growth or physical expansion, but it may just as easily show up as deeper connections to its purpose and greater solidarity with its community. An elevated brand is one in which its systems, staff and success metrics are all in true alignment with its vision and values.

Figure 2.1 **The ACE brand model**

Within each section are six key elements.

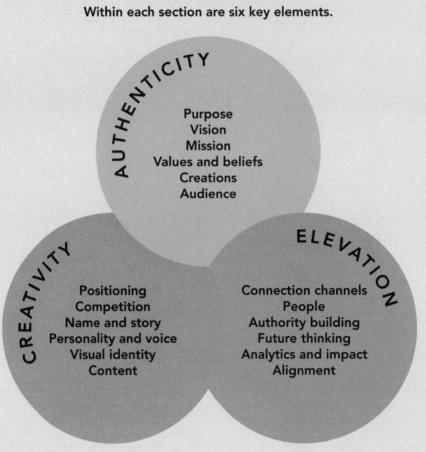

AUTHENTICITY

Purpose
Vision
Mission
Values and beliefs
Creations
Audience

CREATIVITY

Positioning
Competition
Name and story
Personality and voice
Visual identity
Content

ELEVATION

Connection channels
People
Authority building
Future thinking
Analytics and impact
Alignment

What is a brand?

Authenticity

The *authenticity* area of brand comprises purpose, vision, mission, values and beliefs, creations and audience.

1. Purpose

A brand must have a reason for existing. As you have read, creating a business can be done easily and by virtually anyone within moments. But if you want to create something with a deeper meaning behind it, then you have to really understand the purpose of that brand. What do you want to build with this brand? Why are you, the brand leader, excited to be at the helm? What is it trying to do?

2. Vision

What is the big-picture vision for this brand? How can you take it from an unknown entity into something that changes the world? How might it leave the world a little better than before? What does the vision look like now? Five years from now? Twenty years from now?

3. Mission

What is at the heart of the 'what' and 'how' of your business? This is your mission. What are you aiming to achieve right now with this brand? What can you promise your audience today that you know you can deliver on? What are you doing to meet/exceed your objectives and why should anyone care? How does your mission set you apart from everyone else in the market? Which communities can be built around your mission?

4. Values and beliefs

What does your brand stand for? What are the values and beliefs that support its existence and its success well into the future? When people buy into your brand, what are they telling the world around them that they believe in and support? What and who does your brand align with? What and who does it stand opposed to?

5. Creations

Your financials as a brand must work in order to make an impact. What are you creating and why is it important? Is it a product? A service? An experience? A mix of all three? How do your offers reflect the brand? Which offerings will you be adding to the mix now and in years to come? Which gaps are your products or services, or both, closing? What does your pricing strategy look like and how does it impact your overall vision?

6. Audience

Who is your brand serving? Will this change over time? What does life look like for them right now? What do they want life to look like for them and their loved ones in the future? How does your brand help this happen? What are their pains? Their pleasures? Their desires? What drives and motivates them?

Business *to* Brand

Creativity

The *creativity* area of brand comprises positioning, competition, name and story, personality and voice, visual identity, and content.

1. Positioning

As much as every small business owner wants to believe they are their own unique snowflake, the chances that someone else already offers what you do, in a similar way, is high. How will/do you position your brand in the market so that it stands out? Where does the consumer position it when they look at the market for your industry or sector?

2. Competition

Where does your brand sit in the market right now and who else lives in this space? What makes you not only different, but also better than them? What are they doing now that you may do better in the future? How does your ideal audience view you in relation to them? In what areas are you *connecting*, where your competitors are simply *selling*?

3. Name and story

How does your brand name reflect the overall vision of the company and the story behind it? How does the name fit into the type of brand you're building and the type of people you're hoping to connect with? How do you use storytelling to cultivate connection?

4. Personality and voice

Who is your brand? If you had to give it human characteristics, which traits would it possess? How does the brand speak to and engage with its audience/s? Does encountering it feel like a warm hug from a loved one, or a cool nod from a respected leader? What is your brand trying to say? What is its core message? What sort of tone does it possess?

5. Visual identity

What does your brand look like? How does it express itself in typeface, colour palette, photography styling and visual tone? How does it use visual language to tell its story? How do people feel when they view your visuals? How do your visuals come to life in all of your brand touchpoints? How are you utilising design to set up your brand today and well into the future?

6. Content

How will you connect with and engage your audience through content? Which themes are of most interest to them and what subject matter is most important to bring to life your brand and business objectives?

Elevation

The *elevation* area of brand comprises connection channels, people, authority building, future thinking, analytics and impact, and alignment.

1. Connection channels

Which marketing and communication channels will serve you best in connecting with your audience now and into the future? How often will you connect with them and what will be your main medium of message? Which content pillars and themes will be present in your connection points and through what lens will the majority of your communication be channelled?

2. People

It's said that your people are your greatest asset in business, so what are you doing in your brand to not only attract the best possible staff, suppliers and stockists but also to keep them engaged and devoted to the overall vision now, tomorrow and well into the future? How can you ensure that they know what the brand is about from the moment they see a recruitment ad? How do you scale your business sustainably and set your people up for success?

3. Authority building

How will your brand become an authority in the industry or sector you play in? How will you show credibility and build recognition? How will it become known as a trusted brand in your space? What does authority look like for your brand? How will this authority grow and expand in the future?

4. Future thinking

What can you do now to futureproof your business? What might you want to do differently in the future? Which parts of the business will stay on forever and which areas may be removed in time? What is your strategy for continual growth as a brand?

5. Analytics and impact

How will you determine and analyse your elevation as a brand? How will you create a seamless experience both internally and externally? Which metrics will you use to measure your vision and mission? How will you use metrics to understand your audience's needs?

6. Alignment

What is the brand's promise? What is it telling its audience it will deliver on? How will it deliver on this and how will this brand promise be monitored and measured over time, both by those within the brand and those outside of it? What is the brand gap between promise and delivery and how might you close that?

Business *to* Brand

As is becoming evident, a brand is so much more than its visuals. When you consider your own business, how far is it from being a brand? How much, or how little, of the elements listed above have been part of your original business planning or your current strategy? What is the perception your audience has of your brand and how are you working to influence that?

If the answer is more on the side of 'very little', exhale. This is exactly why you have picked up this book and please know that by the end of reading it, and working through the tasks within, you will feel so much more confident – and excited – about creating a brand you're fully in alignment with.

Before we jump into the tasks to consider from this chapter, I want to highlight three important lenses through which to consider your brand:

1. Brand archetypes
2. Brand psychology
3. The buyer cycle.

What is a brand?

Brand archetypes

If you have ever studied psychology or sociology you may well have heard of Carl Jung, the Swiss psychiatrist who in 1919 outlined a series of twelve personality types that he believed every human on the planet could identify with.

Not only could every person fit into one of these twelve types – and display typical behaviours, desires and attributes of that personality type – but characters within films and books, and later brands themselves (as the work of brand strategists and authors Margaret Mark and Carol S Pearson shows), could also be reflected in those archetypes. By fitting into one or two archetypes, a brand can be universally perceived by anyone on earth, regardless of their culture, religion or generation. In that way, the brand became 'human', with a recognisable personality that people could genuinely connect with. We will discuss this again in Chapter 6, but for now, let's get familiar with the concept and archetypes themselves.

The brand archetypes are grouped into four themed quadrants (see Figure 2.2 on page 34).

Seeking paradise

- The Innocent (Safety). Example brand: Dove
- The Sage (Knowledge). Example brand: Google
- The Explorer (Freedom). Example brand: Patagonia

Leaving a legacy

- The Outlaw (Liberation). Example brand: VICE
- The Magician (Transformation). Example brand: Disney
- The Hero (Mastery). Example brand: Nike

Building connection

- The Lover (Intimacy). Example brand: Victoria's Secret
- The Jester (Pleasure). Example brand: M&Ms
- The Everyman (Belonging). Example brand: IKEA

Providing structure

- The Caregiver (Service). Example brand: Thankyou
- The Ruler (Control). Example brand: Rolex
- The Creator (Innovation). Example brand: Apple

Your brand's personality and how it utilises this to attract its audience can usually be married into one or two of the archetypes listed above.

Figure 2.2 **The twelve brand archetypes**

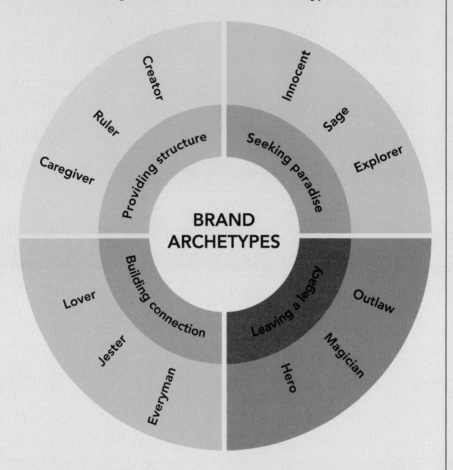

Interesting, isn't it? If it helps, you can pause here and consider five brands you love and find authentic.

- Which archetypes do they best fit?

- Is there a pattern among the brands you have personally connected most with? Do they all fall into the same one or two archetypes?

- Does this have any influence on the brand archetypes you would like your brand to embody?

When you're ready, let's chat about brand psychology.

What is a brand?

Brand psychology

So much of what we connect with in a brand – whether it's the brand behind a food item we consume in seconds or a larger purchase that requires months or even years of contemplation – is personal. The list of elements in the ACE brand framework showcases a range of things that you would also often look for in a partner or friend when forming relationships: What do they value? What beliefs do they hold? What's their style? How do they express themselves? What impact do they have on their friends, family and the community? Why should I want them in my life? How do they improve my day-to-day existence? How do they provide meaning in my world?

In the same way, when we are creating or strengthening our brand, we want our audience/s to feel a deep connection, a personal connection and a human connection.

To do this, branding will often encompass elements of psychology, including but not limited to pattern recognition, sense of belonging and colour psychology.

Let's look at these now.

Pattern recognition

As much as we like to imagine we have complete free will and make up our minds about things based purely on our own independent thought, there are elements of psychology that are common to every single person on the planet and that massively impact the decisions we make.

One of these is the concept of pattern recognition – looking for patterns as a way to trust something or someone.

Consider a reliable friend or person in your life. Chances are part of what makes them reliable is their consistency. Now, consider a friend, partner or person who you can't rely on. While they may still be enjoyable to be around, there is perhaps a level of unease, uncertainty and distrust as their behaviour may change rapidly from day to day and you're never really sure what you're going to get.

Humans use pattern recognition to learn, understand and analyse their environment. Without finding patterns in things, everything would appear new every single time we encountered it and life would feel incredibly stressful. By recognising patterns in the short term we create long-term stories and memories about things in our life, such as 'this is safe' or 'I need to avoid this'. We look for patterns in everything from people's behaviour and physical reactions to foods we eat, through to patterns in architecture and government regulations. Most adults who regularly use a car will understand how to put on a seatbelt regardless of the make or model of the car. Likewise, in many countries we know that green = exit/go and red = don't enter/stop.

Pattern recognition is something we also do when it comes to brands. We seek out consistency in the brand's communication and messages. We begin to trust a brand when it is consistent and meets our expectations, and on the flip side we begin to lose trust when the brand seems unreliable, inauthentic or inconsistent.

Sense of belonging

We have all heard or read stories about ancient peoples and their need to belong to a group for their survival. And we may have also experienced the need to 'fit in' as a teenager. This sense of belonging is a psychological need that can lead us into all sorts of communities and groups throughout our lives.

A sense of belonging can equally lead us to feel attracted to, connect with and buy into various brands. As the custodian of a brand, consider the sense of belonging your brand is encouraging. By engaging with or buying X your audience is expressing Y and therefore feeling a sense of belonging to the community Z. How do you encourage this? How do people retain a sense of belonging when they purchase or even interact with your brand?

One brand that has created a sense of belonging in a sector not usually known for community is the Australian toilet paper brand Who Gives a Crap. Since its inception in 2012 (via a crowdfunding campaign), the brand has almost become a status symbol for those who want to appear to be giving back and supporting creativity (at the time of writing, the brand gives 50% of its profits to help build toilets and improve sanitation in developing countries). By buying Who Gives a Crap toilet paper, these individuals and businesses feel a sense of belonging to a group that wants to do good.

Colour psychology

If you have ever been unlucky enough to have a young child undergo surgery or stay in hospital for any length of time, you'll know that paediatric wards are often places full of bright colours, with murals painted on the walls, animal images or positive affirmations shown in large lettering (or even neon lighting) across arches and doors. The reason for this is to keep the kids (and possibly parents and guardians) positive, hopeful and enjoying their surroundings (as much as one can in this environment). Likewise, if you have ever engaged in a facial or luxurious massage, you'll no doubt have found dimmed lights, pastel colours on the walls and even candlelight being used to evoke a sense of calm and tranquillity.

Colour psychology is the use of colour (including lighting) to help us feel various emotions. Check out any psychology of colour chart (like the one shown in Figure 6.5 on page 164) and you'll find that the colour blue = trust, security and responsibility, which is often why many health insurance companies utilise it. The colour yellow = happiness, optimism, positivity and diversity, which is why it is used in so many childcare centres, youth stores and even fast-food outlets. Sale signs and urgency marketing collateral will often feature the colour red, which is associated with excitement, energy and passion (and emergency vehicles!) and screams, 'This needs my attention!' The choice of colours you bring into your brand collateral, including everything from your logo through to the choice of wall colour in your bathrooms, will speak to your brand message.

These are just a few of the ways that psychology impacts brand. There is also experience, emotional connection, community building and self-awareness. Understanding the power of psychology in branding is essential when transforming your small business into a brand.

Finally, let's chat about …

The buyer cycle

The buyer cycle, also known as the customer journey, sales funnel, customer funnel (and about 1,034,758 other names!), is a cycle that is helpful to keep in mind at every stage of brand-building, marketing and sales.

Now, despite what some on social media may want you to believe, this is not a new concept. Way back in 1898, the American advertising advocate E St Elmo Lewis came up with the idea of a customer journey when he mapped out the stages that a person would take from the moment they were made aware of your brand through to the time they purchased from it. This is known as the AIDA model (Awareness, Interest, Desire, Action).

Many businesses only focus on what they call their sales funnel, which is often represented visually like the diagram below in Figure 2.3.

Figure 2.3 **Funnel framework**

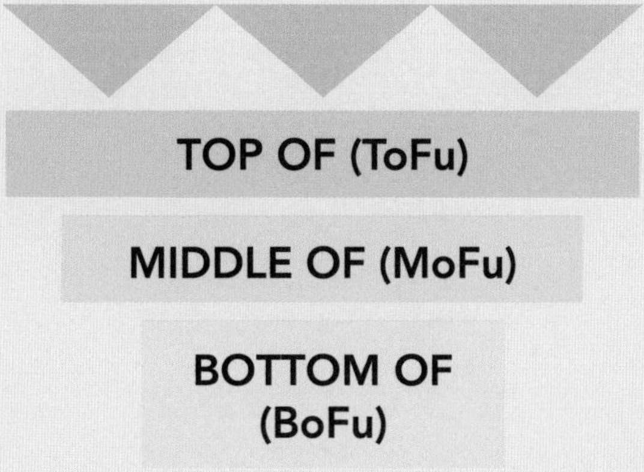

TOP OF (ToFu)

MIDDLE OF (MoFu)

BOTTOM OF (BoFu)

Business *to* Brand

In this framework, the Top of Funnel (ToFu) is where you gather your initial leads or customers. This is the stage of driving awareness and where you might hear people suggesting the use of controversial content matter, collaborations, paid media opportunities and more. (Personally, I don't think being controversial purely for the sake of it is a great philosophy, but you do you.)

The second stage is the Middle of Funnel (yep the MoFu, which could well mean something entirely different!) which is all about driving consideration and evaluation. This is where your leads become more qualified and excited to turn into prospects.

The last stage, the Bottom of Funnel (BoFu), is about driving decision-making and conversion. This is where you're going hard to sell and get people who have travelled all the way down the funnel to commit.

The reason I don't love this framework – particularly when you're building a brand – is because it tends to spit people out and is all about one end goal, rather than seeing the possibilities for more. I like to compare this to a one-night stand (which can be some people's way of running a business – got the sale, thanks, byeee!) vs building a genuine connection and forming relationships through your brand.

The framework I like to use and will ask you to consider multiple times in this book, and long after you have finished it, is the buyer cycle (see Figure 2.4 on the opposite page). This is a more customer-centric way of doing things, because I believe brands need to be more customer and connection focused.

Controversial? Not trying to be. Let's just be human.

Figure 2.4 **The buyer cycle**

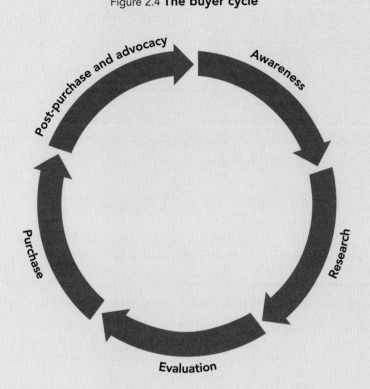

The cycle has no end and is all about nurturing people and keeping them in your community to engage with again and again and again. While some of that engagement may result in financial gain, the purpose of a brand here is to create loyalty and authentic connection so that even if they never buy again there is still a genuine relationship built.

Business *to* Brand

The buyer cycle has six key stages and each stage needs the prior one to be well executed and to create a good experience in order to achieve the next. I want to point out that this cycle can be applied to anything you transact with – from buying a house through to looking for a new synagogue or mosque in your area (think joining, not purchasing).

Let's look at each of these stages.

AWARENESS

This is when people first become aware of your business or brand. This may come about in any number of ways, from you being interviewed on a podcast through to a friend wearing your product to a barbecue and someone asking where it's from. Someone has moved from never knowing about you to now being aware of you.

If they feel inspired or inclined they will move into the next stage of …

RESEARCH

This is where they will take on the task of discovering more. This may be putting your name into a Google search or a social media platform, asking people in their network and communities questions, coming into your physical location or browsing your website. It is at this stage that they are looking for key pieces of information – what do you offer and how does it apply to the problem they are trying to solve?

If they have found sufficient information and are still interested in the brand's offer, they may well move into the stage of …

EVALUATION

It is in this evaluation stage that people may compare your business or brand to others, looking for evidence of values alignment, or looking for ways in which your brand helps them identify with parts of themselves (e.g. social enterprise helps me feel good about myself, an ethical supply chain helps me feel I'm doing my part). It's also in this stage that they may be looking for ways that your brand helps them to help others. This is one of the most important phases in the buyer cycle as after this stage is 'ticked', it's really about creating a smooth and easy path to purchase.

Once someone has passed through this stage, it's on to …

PURCHASE

As the name suggests, this is where the *cha-ching!* happens and where someone has decided that your brand is the right choice. Ensuring that the path to purchase aligns with your brand values, caters to the needs of your audience and, most importantly, is simple to execute is crucial for your brand's continued success. This is where so many businesses and brands can inject a hefty dose of frustration into their audiences by either failing to qualify people before this step (e.g. a landscape architect only works with people who have a budget of $100K+ and above but doesn't communicate this anywhere until the point of purchase which leads to time being wasted on both sides) or adding something surprising (and not in a good way) such as mammoth shipping fees that wipe out the excitement of purchase.

It's at this stage that many business owners will stop analysing, which sucks for them as the next step can be the most lucrative for businesses – both financially and emotionally. Strong brands know that much of the relationship nurturing will happen at the stage of ...

POST-PURCHASE

I pointed out in Chapter 1 that it takes about ten times the marketing costs to attain a new customer or client than it does to retain someone who has bought from you previously. It is in this post-purchase stage that your greatest strengthening of relationships can happen. This is your after-care information, your 'in case you missed it' communications, your request to see a photo of your brand's products in their home, and the connection you continue to build after the point of purchase.

If this stage is done well, it can guide people to the next stage of ...

ADVOCACY

This is where you have a bunch of people who love what your brand offers and the experience they have had with you that they actively choose to share their thoughts and feelings with friends, family and – if you're lucky – their wider networks. We are social creatures and this is where social proof can be incredibly powerful. Once someone is an advocate they are actively encouraging others to come into your orbit, become aware of the business and begin their own journey in the buyer cycle with your brand.

When it comes to building a brand, there is a lot to consider. On one hand, it's simple stuff – be genuine, show up, know what you're trying to do, who it benefits and remain consistent. On the other, when we are constantly being bombarded with get-rich-quick schemes and mass production made with zero consideration for human and environmental welfare, it can perhaps feel difficult and overwhelming to jump out of the rat race and actually create something that matters.

It's my hope that by the end of this book you will understand that building a brand is really just a simple, human approach to creating something meaningful with your business.

'A brand today must be absolutely clear on its vision – what it is trying to achieve in the long term – as well as who it is for. It must understand and authentically align with its values – the guiding principles that impact its offerings and its marketing and connection channels.'

What is a brand?

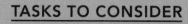

TASKS TO CONSIDER

Before getting stuck into Chapter 3, where you will take an honest look at how your current or future brand is performing, it's time to take a moment and cement the learnings from this chapter.

Work through the following questions or download them in a worksheet form online via the QR code below.

1.   What resonated most with you from this chapter? Why?

2.   Were there any parts of the brand's history that surprised you?

3.   How many elements in the ACE brand model do you feel your business has considered, documented and aligned itself with?

4.   When you began your business (or came up with the idea of it), which brand elements were the most exciting for you? And the least exciting?

5.   Which of the brand elements are you least confident in? Why is this?

6.   Which psychological elements does your brand already engage in? Which might you like to learn more about or implement more of?

7.   How far/close is your business to becoming an ACE brand?

Before we jump into Chapter 3, we'll hear from Becca Stern who together with her sister Jess Stern created their globally adored colourful brand Mustard.

Scan for digital worksheet

Business *to* Brand

Image: Zoe Lonergan (zoelonergan.com)

*'It's important to
remember that building
a brand means
building something
bigger than you.
You are the custodian,
you are not your brand.'*

Profile: *Mustard*

What started as a way of keeping two sisters (living in Australia and the UK) connected through a joint business venture has become the much loved and globally successful brand Mustard, which counts celebrities, designers and everyday colour enthusiasts among its loyal following. Created in 2018 by Becca and Jess Stern, the brand has become synonymous with colourful content, joyful storytelling and a way of bringing the fun back into life. Here's what co-founder Becca Stern had to say about building a brand.

How would you sum up Mustard?

We create pretty and practical products that help people design colourful, organised and inspiring spaces.

What do you believe is the difference between running a business and being the custodian of a brand?

For me, most of what falls under the umbrella of 'business' is transactional. It's the nuts and bolts, the day-to-day. The business is what we do, whereas the brand is who we are. I say that in the sense that who we are is Mustard, because it's also important to remember that building a brand means building something bigger than you. You are the custodian, you are not your brand. If you see yourself and your brand as a single entity you're layering all your personal aspirations but also limitations onto your business.

Mustard is a separate entity to 'Becca' and 'Jess', and we think creating that delineation is a really important boundary to hold if we want Mustard to be the best brand it can possibly be, and to have a sustainable future.

Did you consider Mustard a brand from the start?

Absolutely. We were clear that we wanted to create something bigger than simply the products we were designing. We knew we wanted our business to have longevity, focus, personality and a sense of clarity in terms of our voice. The business was designed with scalability in mind, though we really didn't anticipate the proportions or speed of the growth from the beginning. Before we launched at a trade show in Sydney, I had developed a business plan with two-year projections. In that first weekend alone, we exceeded those figures! That was a real wake-up call that we needed to dream bigger.

Mustard seemed to go global so quickly. How do you think this happened?

It helps when one co-founder lives in Australia and the other lives in the UK! The business was set up to be global from the get-go. We've been fortunate that living on opposite sides of the world gave us an opportunity to learn the ropes and to each steer the business in two locations. For the first year it was just the two of us which meant we got to know every facet of the business before hiring and handing over areas as our team grew. We launched in Australia in February 2018 and in the UK in September that year. The skills and processes we learnt from having two regions gave us the confidence to stretch further into the US and Europe.

One of our most important learnings has been to build the scalability to go global into our business from the start. When we first launched Mustard, my initial idea was to do our shipping and logistics myself from a container in our backyard. Thank goodness we scrapped that idea and found a 3PL (third-party logistics) partner because there is no way we could have scaled and grown into the global brand we are today if we had taken that approach.

Launching globally is a risk, whether you're familiar with the market or not, but it can be a calculated one. I'd say do your research, and test, test, test – just because something works in one region, doesn't mean it will in others. You also don't have to do it alone – and you really shouldn't! Other people have been there before and can help guide you. So reach out, ask questions and enlist people who know the area.

What have been some of the best things you have done to grow the brand over the years?

There's a saying that your brand is what people say about you when you're not in the room. From that perspective, the most important thing we've done to grow our brand is to build great relationships. We have amazing rapport with our stockists. We've tried to create a workplace our team loves. We offer the absolute best customer experience. We show up on our social channels authentically. If we do all of this in alignment with our values, the things people say about us when we're not in the room will reflect the vision of the brand we're crafting.

To that point, the second most important thing is consistency. We want everyone who interacts with Mustard to have an experience that reflects our brand and values, whether that's through an Instagram post or purchasing a product. We have a clearly defined tone of voice, and a look and feel that is distinctly Mustard. We invest (and have from very early on) in very high-quality imagery of our products and of ourselves (this really helps with press opportunities!). We are fanatics for a consistent Insta feed. And we constantly, actively use our brand values as a filter.

What do you think the biggest myth is around the idea of building a brand today?

That a brand is a logo and colour palette. It is so much deeper and longer term. Values are such a core part of building a brand, and that's something we've seen in action. When we first launched we thought lockers would be a one-time purchase, but it turns out that's (luckily) not the case at all. Many of our customers are repeat buyers, lockers are definitely addictive! I think that's partly due to our values and how we talk about them. People like knowing who they're supporting with their purchase, and what that means.

I also think the pressure to always have something 'new' is a bit of a myth. You don't have to jump on every trend or launch a new product every season. Do what you do, do it really well, and stay in your lane.

What legacy would you like Mustard to leave behind?

For me personally, something that always motivates me is that I want to set a good example for my children. I want them to know that you can be strong and soft, that you can dream big and achieve great things while being kind and having good values. I want them to be proud of what I have created and to know they can be brave and forge their own path too.

For Mustard, a huge part of the legacy we're building is our involvement with Beam, a not-for-profit based in the UK that supports people experiencing homelessness to find safe housing, jobs and training opportunities.

We're Beam's largest corporate sponsor; as a still relatively small and new business, that's an achievement I'm really proud of.

How often do you/the team review the brand and its vision and strategy? How do you do this?

In the first few years of Mustard, our team was tiny so a lot of the vision and the strategy was largely in our heads. Things moved so quickly, but we always felt like we were on the same page. Now we have a team and hope to inspire and lead them, things look a little different and we've had to evolve and formalise our processes.

At the start of the year we had an intense month of strategy with the two of us and our husbands (who now work with us in Mustard). The outcome was a beautiful, clear set of focuses, our 'big rocks'. This is a document we refer to all the time and it's been filtered through all areas of the business and our team. We've also found it beneficial for sharing with external partners to help them see what our priorities are and where we are headed.

One of my mottos is 'as this business grows, we need to grow too'. This was a big step forward for me and for the whole of Mustard. Now that we have hired a team of people who are experts in their own fields it's given me the scope to take my hands off the day-to-day and to step into the role of leader. My role now is to set and hold the vision, to help direct the rest of the team and steer the brand.

It can be easy for someone on the outside to think you must have known exactly what you were doing, at all times, for you to have such a successful and respected global brand. What have been some of the challenges?

We definitely didn't (and don't) always know what we were doing! There have certainly been quite a few bumps in the road. We've had fires on shipping containers, stock stuck in the Suez Canal for weeks,

Brexit interrupting our shipping to Europe, customs dramas and copycat products to name a few!

In all these moments, our solutions have come in the form of the great relationships we have built (along with some really late nights!). Having strong communication and understanding with our key partners, in our 3PL and factory especially, has saved the day more than once. We also make it a priority to be clear and transparent with our customers. With 'honest' being a core value, when times are challenging, we always communicate openly and honestly, bringing our customers on the journey with us.

What's the best business advice you have received that you wish you had known when you were starting your brand?

I'm a big lover of quotes and I recently found an old proverb that resonates with my experience as an entrepreneur: 'I'm a great believer in luck, and I find the harder I work, the more I have of it.' I personally love the challenge of running a business, it is all-consuming, unpredictable and bloody hard work. I have found it's so important to embrace the hard bits, to see them as part of your job description and when things get messy, it helps to remember that it's because you are doing something worthwhile. Jess and I have always called it 'swimming in the deep end' – there's nowhere else I'd rather be!

Why do you think building a brand, and not simply a business, is important today?

Starting a business is more accessible than ever these days. You can pretty much design and order any product, from anywhere in the world. So if you don't have the strength of a brand to carry the business, it's much harder to stand out in the market. What we're selling is not just a product, it's our brand. It's the connection people have to Mustard, to us as the faces behind the brand, and it's the reason they come back again and again and fill their lives with lockers.

Web: mustardmade.com

IG: @mustardmade

TT: @mustardmadelockers

Image: Zoe Lonergan (zoelonergan.com)

Business *to* Brand

03.

Where are you now?

Sometime towards the end of 2017, while my husband and I were discussing what we hoped 2018 would bring for us, he made a suggestion. It was the kind of suggestion that anyone in a long-term relationship might find surprising. I could tell he was nervous and there was a lengthy pause before I figured out what I would say in reply. Now, before you let your mind go to all sorts of raunchy places, slow your roll.

My husband's suggestion was that we both give up alcohol.

For at least twelve months. Um … okay.

At the time we had an almost four year old and we were both devoted to the idea of growing our family with a second child. Up until that point, despite our best efforts, it just wasn't happening. Anyone who has spent time trying to conceive without the results they had hoped for knows how heartbreaking and mentally exhausting the process can be. Prior to this particular conversation we had both agreed that 2018 would be the final year of trying. Should we not fall pregnant that year we would count our blessings with the one much-loved child we had and move on.

Which brings me back to my husband's suggestion.

Seeing the surprise (read: fear?) in my eyes he said, 'It would make sense to give up alcohol, along with coffee, get healthier and just know we have given it our best shot.'

As someone who grew up in Australia and as a child of Irish parents, I definitely enjoyed a wine or two. In my late teens and throughout my twenties, alcohol was just a part of my life – whether it was a few glasses of wine alongside a cheeseboard and beautiful conversations with close friends or a glass of my favoured Bacardi and Diet Coke sipped while dancing up a storm on the podium of my favourite nightclubs circa 1998. As a mum of a young child, a new business owner trying to grow my brand and a devoted daughter with ageing parents, I dealt with the stress in the way a lot of people do. As much as it feels awkward to admit, I used wine as a way of relaxing. A few years prior to this, I had taken to only having wine on the weekend and I would love watching the clock hit 5 pm on a Friday and opening up a crisp and cold bottle of white wine.

While I understood where my husband was coming from, I can't say that agreeing to a year of zero alcohol felt super appealing. That said, in the hope of gaining another child, I was willing to do virtually anything.

Whether or not abstaining from drinking was helpful in falling pregnant with our second child the next September, I'll never know, but what I did find was a far better quality of sleep, clearer skin and eyes, and greater clarity of thought. I carried on not drinking for the first few months of my new child's life; it was easy as I was breastfeeding and tired, and didn't want anything to interrupt what little sleep I was able to get.

By the time you'll be reading this my second child will be five and a half years old and I will probably have had a total of one or two glasses of wine since I started my serious 2018 quest-to-fall-pregnant journey with him. For someone who used to drink multiple times a week, this is a pretty big deal. This isn't to boast or project my personal choices onto anyone else – if you want to drink that's entirely up to you – but to say that it is possible to change and move in a new direction.

Where are you now?

Anyone that knew me in my younger years would perhaps be shocked that I no longer drink. Heck, I find myself shocked by it sometimes, too.

In the same way, changing your small business into a more holistic and meaningful brand can feel incredibly scary. Making the necessary changes to move in a new direction or standing up for a cause publicly may feel surprising to some of your closest friends and family. Perhaps you're worried about alienating your current audience by changing course or even fearful of the response from within the business, from staff or long-serving suppliers or manufacturers.

I have worked with thousands of small business owners over the last decade and many still worry about how their friends, family and/or peers will perceive something they do in their business. Or they feel anxious about the response to a change in strategy or tactics from staff. When you're employed it's easy to distance yourself from your employer. When you run your own business so much of what the business does or stands for is a direct reflection of your own beliefs and values.

Change is rarely comfortable. If it was, more people would jump right in to change things in their health, personal lives, relationships and, yes, in their business. Change can be incredibly hard and awkward and confronting. Giving up alcohol was something that not only impacted me, but also impacted some of the people closest to me who saw in my choices perhaps their own dependence on drinking to relax. In the same way, when you decide to move from a business to a brand and do the necessary deep work in really understanding the impact your brand is or will be having on the world, the values and beliefs that guide it, the ways of working you want to do more (and less) of and the reasons it exists at all, it may well hold a mirror up to other friends/peers in business, or your own audience/s, who see in your change perhaps their own hopes and ambitions unrealised.

George Bernard Shaw suggested: 'Progress is impossible without change.' When it comes to moving from a business into a brand, change is one of the main ingredients for success, not only in the original transition but also throughout the entire lifetime of the brand.

I debated whether or not to include my story about changes in my personal life, but in this chapter I'll be asking you to be really honest, so I may as well start that way myself.

Why *honesty*?

Because in this chapter, I want you to closely consider where you are right now and where you would like to be in the future. Building a brand – and retaining genuine authenticity – is something that takes a great deal of honesty and commitment and standing strong when it feels easier to let go of what you say you stand for. Building a brand that matters is about challenging yourself, questioning your integrity and making sure that necessary changes are made and that your values are adhered to. It's about being honest with yourself on what you're trying to accomplish with your brand and why.

As your brand grows – by whichever metrics you deem important – you will need to test that honesty and be clear on whether you are showing up authentically. Building an authentic brand demands assessment at every stage and you can only do that by getting really honest. So take a deep breath and let's get started.

Simon Sinek is often seen as the Godfather for the idea of 'why' when it comes to business (if you don't know who he is, watch his now-famous TED Talk on discovering your 'why'), but as you have read in the brief history of brand, the idea of there being a 'meaning' behind a brand has been around for decades.

What is the meaning behind your brand?

What impact do you want it to have on the world?

Why, apart from any financial gain, did you start your business?

These may seem like simple questions, but they can be some of the hardest to answer, especially if you began your business as a side project and it grew quickly without you having to consider all of the above. Perhaps you had an idea originally but the business has grown and changed over the years (or even decades) and now you're unsure as to its real impact. Or perhaps you have ignored questions like these previously, feeling they were a little 'fluffy'. If you haven't yet figured these answers out, I would urge you to take the time to do so.

How?

The first thing to consider is your time on this planet. Time is something none of us – even the Beyoncés of the world – can make more of. When it's gone, it's gone. It may seem like a deep question in a business book, but what impact do you wish to make with your time while you still have it?

When I started my own business, at the end of 2015, I wanted to give creative people a choice over how they made money. I saw too many friends stressed out, overwhelmed and falling into states of depression and anxiety because they were spending the majority of their working hours (and adult life) in a job they hated. Or they had started a business and it simply became another job they hated.

Think about it: most of us start working sometime in our mid to late teens – I was at the check-outs at our local supermarket at fourteen years and nine months (at the time, the earliest you could start working in Australia). Most people will then work until they are in their seventies (or later, depending on the pension schemes they may or may not have available). That's not only the majority of our lives, but also the majority of time when we will be in our greatest health, have some of our most meaningful relationships and be able to do things like travel, exercise, volunteer and spend time in nature on our own terms. If the average person works forty hours a week from fifteen to seventy years of age, that's a total of 114,400 hours working – a huge amount of time to hate what you do, or to feel like it's contributing little to your community and the world at large.

Prior to starting my own business, I was working as Head of Marketing for a brand I wasn't super proud to attach my name to. I was working around the clock (think 6.30 am starts and 11 pm finishes) and giving up time with my young son, my husband and my ageing parents. I was also neglecting my health, my spirituality and my capacity to volunteer in my community. Now, I know it is an incredible privilege to have the choice to consider starting a business, let alone quitting a 'secure' job (like the one I had) to go out on an uncertain path like entrepreneurship. I also know how many women in my ancestry would have cherished the opportunity to make their own money doing something they loved, and how hard the generations before me fought for the freedoms so many of us now take for granted.

Where are you now?

I wanted to start my own business to share the knowledge I had gained over fifteen years working in brand, content and marketing for some of the most innovative companies in the world with people who wanted to start their own creative businesses. I wanted to alleviate the feeling in my friends and peers that work always had to equate to something they loathed ('Isn't that just life?'). I wanted to show them how to make a decent income and set up structures to support this in a sustainable way while still having time for things they found important such as family, health, creative endeavours and nature. I wanted them to spend those 100,000 plus hours of their life feeling like they were doing something they were proud of, contributing to the world in a way they could feel engaged and excited by, and making enough money to sustain the rest of their life along the way.

The meaning behind my own brand was to give people freedom and choice. This is still a huge part of My Daily Business and impacts the offers we have, the way my team and I work, and the choices we make when it comes to connection channels, collaborations and partnerships, and content themes. Our businesses are such a huge part of our lives today. The purpose of my brand is to help people figure out ways to enjoy both business and life, on the daily.

Perhaps your purpose is to create more sustainable pathways to production, with natural resources and less impact on the environment. Perhaps it is to innovate and change the way people think and engage with a certain industry or sector. Perhaps your brand teaches people how to become more self-aware, thereby changing the lens through which they parent, love or create. Perhaps your brand is all about empowering groups that have historically been victimised, oppressed or abused. Perhaps it's about bringing awe and beauty into the everyday.

There are *many* reasons why a brand exists and you should spend time figuring out yours. As discussed, competition is in abundance in today's market with copycat businesses being created in seconds. One of the biggest ways to set yourself apart is to share the why behind your business, your unique reasons for existing and the impact you wish your brand to have on the world now and well into the future.

If you're finding it difficult to get clarity on your 'why', consider the following exercises.

Legacy

The first exercise is to think about the idea of legacy and what you want to leave behind.

I have been fortunate to have had two amazing and loving parents for the first thirty-five years of my life. I have been unfortunate to have lost both in the last few years (along with my beloved father-in-law). In addition to this, I lost my best friend to a horrific car accident when she was just twenty-one. While death is the only certainty we have, it is one we will forever be shocked by. One of the most beautiful things we can do for those we lose is to acknowledge their lives and legacy in eulogies and the way we celebrate their life after it's been lived. I will forever be grateful to my eldest sibling, who captured our parents' full lives in wonderful eulogies that spoke to their gifts, their passions, their love, their humour and their purpose. It is an almost impossible task to sum up decades of life in a ten-minute speech, but he did so beautifully.

You're probably wondering what this has to do with building a brand?

It may seem strange, but one exercise that can help you gain clarity on your brand's meaning and purpose is to consider its impact after its existence. Imagine, for a moment, that your brand had an incredible run – think thirty successful years or more. It did exactly what you had set out as its original purpose. What would the eulogy for your brand say? How might you sum up its impact on the world in a succinct manner? How did it start? How did it elevate? How will it continue to have an impact on its audience/s long after it's passed away?

Ask 'why?'

The second exercise is to get to the heart of a brand's purpose by continually asking the simple one-word question: *Why?*

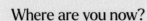

I first heard about this on a mindfulness podcast where a Buddhist monk suggested that when we feel misaligned we should keep asking ourselves 'Why?' over and over and over until we get to the heart of the problem (if you have ever been around a toddler, you'll know exactly how this goes).

For example:

I am feeling angry. *Why?*

Because I was left out of the invitation to XYZ and it pissed me off. *Why?*

Because I always feel left out and it makes me sad. *Why?*

Because it makes me feel like I'm of no value to anyone and that's not a nice feeling. *Why?*

Because isn't life supposed to be about connection? I don't feel connected right now. *Why?*

Because I don't feel close to my family and I feel unloved. *Why?*

Because maybe I'm not lovable. *Why?*

Because maybe I'm broken and no one will ever love me.

That last line is the core of the root of the problem (I feel broken vs I'm angry that someone forgot to invite me to something). In the same way, you can use the *Why?* questioning as a tactic for clarity when it comes to brand purpose.

For example:

I am going to share my knowledge with others who want to start/scale their business. *Why?*

Because the learnings could help them. *Why?*

Because too many people work jobs they hate and I don't like that. *Why?*

Because life should be at least somewhat enjoyable and so many people don't enjoy it. *Why?*

Because they feel they have no choice about how they make money. *Why?*

Because they need money and they are stuck in a job they hate in order to make that money, which could lead to depression or anxiety or other mental ill health. *Why?*

Because so many of us are taught to go to school, get a job and not complain, and I want to change that by helping them see that they have agency over their lives. *Why?*

Because then they can have the freedom and choice to decide how they spend their time and not feel stuck or depressed. *Why?*

Because this will mean they may have more meaningful and purpose-led lives and that's important. *Why?*

Because it will teach the next generation that you can make money and find fulfilment, and that they're not mutually exclusive. This is important for an individual's own mental health and the entire community around them. *Why?*

Because when more people are happy and enjoy what they do regularly, they have more energy to help others and give back. When people are more content, the world will be in a better place.

It's that last line – 'the world will be in a better place' – that is at the core of this brand's existence. Think about the reason you started your business and the brand you wished to create. Use the question of 'Why?' to get to the deepest reasons behind its existence.

SWOT analysis

Something that can help you figure out your 'why' (and really should be something you're doing regularly when running a business) is a basic SWOT analysis.

SWOT is an acronym that stands for **S**trengths, **W**eaknesses, **O**pportunities and **T**hreats. The SWOT analysis is thought to have been developed by Albert Humphrey at the Stanford Research Institute (SRI) in the 1960s.

Figure 3.1 **SWOT analysis**

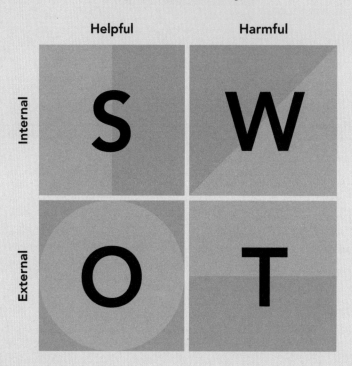

Using the table in Figure 3.2 (page 59), map the strengths, weaknesses, opportunities and threats for your business as it currently stands using the following questions as prompts.

Where are you now?

Under **strengths** you'll be answering these questions:

- What are our current strengths? What do we do really well?
- What are we recognised and respected for?
- Why do customers/clients keep coming back?
- What advantages do we have?
- Which positive traits stand out about our business?
- What are we naturally good at?
- How have we garnered this for better business?
- What are we most proud of?

Under **weaknesses** you'll be answering these questions:

- Why and where have we lost customers/clients?
- Where are the gaps in our knowledge?
- Which processes haven't been set up for success?
- Where could our resources be improved?
- Where are we falling short of our customers'/clients' expectations?
- Where do our competitors do a better job than us?
- Where are we lacking confidence?

Under **opportunities** you'll be answering these questions:

- What will our customers/clients want five years from now?
- How could we get there in two years?
- How might we innovate more?
- How might we utilise technology to improve the business?
- Where are the gaps in what our competitors are offering?
- What have our customers/clients told us they want more of?
- How might we take existing strengths and apply them to new categories or offerings?

Business *to* Brand

Under **threats** you'll be answering these questions:

- Which external forces may hinder our plans right now?
- How might technology impact our top offers/products?
- How might our weaknesses be deepened?
- Are there any economic trends that could negatively impact our business?
- Are there any social trends that could negatively impact our business?
- Are we relying too heavily on one SKU/product/offer for all of our revenue?
- Where is our risk too great right now?
- Are we building a business that can be sustained via systems and not just certain people?
- What would happen if we lost our top staff? How might this impact the business?

Keep your SWOT analysis of your current business somewhere you can refer back to as you work through this book.

Now consider the following questions:

- If you had to choose just ONE area to focus on right now for the business, based on what you have just input into your SWOT, which would it be?
- Is there a strength that could be more fully realised?
- Is there a strength you know you have, but your brand is not yet known for?
- Is there a weakness that is continuing to hamper your brand ambitions?
- Is there an opportunity you can jump on ahead of any competitors?
- Is there an opportunity that highlights a gap in the marketplace?
- Is there a threat that needs to be addressed for your brand to flourish?
- How does your 'why' show up in your strengths and the opportunities you have identified?

Once you have clarity on the impact you want your brand to have on the world and the reasons for its existence, it's time to get honest with yourself on how far or close you are to that reality right now.

Where are you now?

Figure 3.2 **SWOT analysis for my current business**

STRENGTHS	WEAKNESSES

OPPORTUNITIES	THREATS

Business *to* Brand

Where is your brand at today?

If you think back to when you started your business and the purpose you had for it, how close are you to fulfilling that purpose every day? If you were suddenly assessed on the alignment between your brand mission and the daily reality of the business, how would you score?

Using the line in Figure 3.3, score your brand from Basic Business (purely a transactional way for someone to buy X product with no emotional connection) through to Beloved Brand (where your customers are your best brand ambassadors and advocate for everything you put out, from content to product).

Figure 3.3 **My current brand is:**

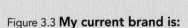

Beloved Brand

Basic Business

Now consider why you gave that score.

- Is it that people don't know the reasons behind why your brand exists?
- Is your purpose something you have kept hidden and never shared?
- Is your purpose mentioned or shown anywhere in your brand collateral?
- Is your purpose obvious to people who buy from or work with you? Why/Why not?

Next, consider where you would ideally like to end up in the next twelve months. Mark it on the line in Figure 3.4 on the opposite page.

Figure 3.4 **My future brand will be:**

Basic Business   **Beloved Brand**

Now consider:

• When you look at this score, how does it make you *feel*?

• What will you need to change to get there?

• How realistic do you think these changes are?

• Which fears arise when you consider this mark on the scale?

Now it's time to consider the key elements of your brand. Take the time to review each of the brand elements then, using the scoring key below, mark where your brand currently sits for each in the table in Figure 3.5 (page 62).

1. I/We have never considered this.

2. I/We have considered, but not begun this.

3. I/We are in the process of creating this.

4. I/We have this, but need to rework it.

5. I/We are well on the way to finalising this.

6. I/We have aced this entirely.

Figure 3.5 **Benchmarks for your brand today**

SECTION	ELEMENT	1	2	3	4	5	6
A (Authenticity)	Purpose						
	Vision						
	Mission						
	Values and beliefs						
	Creations						
	Audience						
C (Creativity)	Positioning						
	Competition						
	Name and story						
	Personality and voice						
	Visual identity						
	Content						
E (Elevation)	Connection channels						
	People						
	Authority building						
	Future thinking						
	Analytics and impact						
	Alignment						

Where are you now?

After completing the table, consider how you feel.

- Are you further behind than you imagined?

- Are you further ahead?

- Which fears or worries are surfacing for you?

- Which element/s feels like it will be the greatest challenge? Why?

It is important at this stage to bring up an element that will either make your business one you absolutely enjoy being a part of or something that will eat away at your soul until you feel like a shell of your former self.

Alignment.

A line that has always stuck with me is from one of my favourite authors, the late Irish poet John O'Donohue: 'One of the deepest longings of the human soul is to be seen.'

In today's world, one way in which we can show who we are is to start a business or brand. We may have a love for the country we were raised in but no longer live in and so we start a homeware business importing artisan pieces made by women in low socio-economic areas of our homeland. Or we may have a deep belief that nature is healing and so we start a business helping people move through grief through hiking and outdoor retreats.

When the business that we start is in alignment with our values and beliefs, in who we believe ourselves to be, we feel seen, valued and productive in terms of our community and the world at large. On the flip side, when we are running a business and attempting to run a brand that doesn't align with our values and beliefs, we retreat into ourselves, not wanting to be seen nor have the business succeed because of this jarring misalignment.

When you consider your own business, how aligned is it to your values and beliefs? To the vision you have for the world around you? How does it help contribute to you feeling like you have done something meaningful? How, like O'Donohue says, does it let you be *seen*?

Now that we have started with a little honesty, it's time to go deeper.

But before you jump into the next section, make sure you have the time and space to dedicate yourself to answering what will be asked of you. This is one of the most important sections of the book, as it will help guide you on the journey from business to brand. To get the most out of it, you have to be willing to be completely honest. This section is not one that you'll want to rush through, so if you're reading this surrounded by people or noise, or both, consider bookmarking it for a time when you can think more clearly. Likewise, if you have been battling a huge task or deadline, consider pausing this and coming back to it when you have the energy to really take on board the questions and connect with your most honest answer. As Thomas Jefferson once said, 'Honesty is the first chapter in the book of wisdom'.

Consider your current business and all of its elements. Then take the time to digest the questions in the Honesty Questionnaire and answer them as authentically as you can. Keep your answers somewhere you can refer back to.

Where are you now?

The Honesty Questionnaire

1. What do I absolutely love about my business?

2. Which parts of the business am I most passionate about?

3. What embarrasses me or makes me squirm about my current business?

4. Which parts of the business feel misaligned with my purpose?

5. If I could sell the business tomorrow, at a fair price, would I? Why/Why not?

6. If my business where a celebrity/well-known figure, who would it be and why?

7. If my business were an animal, what would it be and why?

8. What frustrates me most about my business?

9. How have I, as its founder, contributed to that?

10. Does my business have a strong enough foundation or base to become a brand?

11. Which fears do I hold when it comes to transforming my business into a brand?

12. Am I scared or excited to really have the business (and brand) be seen?

13. What do I wish I had done differently when I started?

14. Which brands do I look up to? Why?

15. Which brands do I really detest? Why?

Remember, there is no right or wrong way to answer these questions. Your business is exactly that – *your business* – and these answers are there to help guide you as you continue to work through this book.

Business *to* Brand

Feel like this is all a bit overwhelming?

Exhale. This is a completely natural way to feel at this stage in your journey.

Creating a brand isn't something you can simply do in the space of one afternoon, as much as it may appear so with online graphics tools and the speed at which a domain can be bought and a website created. Building a brand that is meaningful to both your audience and yourself takes time to digest, analyse, create and figure out. Think of the stage you're at right now as akin to kicking around in an ocean. The sand and shells are coming to the surface and things feel murky, but in time it will clear and you'll be able to see where you're standing again.

The questions you have worked through in this chapter, and those still to come, will test and challenge you. There's no easy way around that; you have to go through it. But, remember, they will also engage you and get you excited about what's possible. Building a brand is a privilege and it is a responsibility to recognise that privilege and use it wisely.

Brands can have a massive impact on their community and, often, on the world at large. Taking the time now to answer these questions will help you create a brand you can absolutely be proud of.

If you're feeling overwhelmed at this stage, remember there is no gold star for finishing early. A brand is like any good relationship, changing and growing as time goes on. For this reason, you want to take your time, really consider your answers and give your brand the time and dedication it deserves if it is to take up a place in the world and have a real impact on the people who engage with it.

Where are you now?

TASKS TO CONSIDER

This has been a chunky chapter with loads of questions – some which you may have answered with ease, and others which may have caused a little more tension to surface. Creating a brand that has purpose, meaning and depth takes time and can't be rushed.

Using what you have learned so far, work through the following questions or download them in a worksheet form online via the QR code below.

1. *What resonated most with you from this chapter? Why?*

2. *Work through figures 3.2 and 3.5 and ensure you have clarity on these. You'll be coming back to them – particularly Figure 3.5 – in later chapters. You may want to bookmark these pages for ease of reference.*

3. *Work through the Honesty Questionnaire and keep your answers somewhere you can refer back to them.*

4. *How has your business allowed you to be 'seen' to date?*

5. *How aligned has your business been with your beliefs and values to date?*

6. *What are the current weaknesses and threats of your business and how might you change these within the brand you're building?*

This was a big chapter! Well done for getting through it. Now it's time to get into the specifics of the brand elements and consider the steps you'll be taking to bring these to life in your own brand.

Before we jump into Chapter 4 will hear from Arjen Klingenberg, the Creative Director and brand guru at Tony's Chocolonely.

Scan for digital worksheet

Business *to* Brand

Image: Studio Mals (studiomals.com)

Profile:
Tony's Chocolonely

Tony's Chocolonely, founded in 2005 in Amsterdam, is a pioneering chocolate company with a mission to make chocolate 100% slave-free. Inspired by the belief that chocolate should be a force for good, Tony's Chocolonely produces delicious, ethically sourced chocolate bars and snacks. They lead the industry in transparency, partnering with cocoa farmers and advocating for fair wages and sustainable farming practices. Here's what Creative Director and brand guru Arjen Klinkenberg had to say about the brand.

'*Why does this company exist in the first place? It's this "why" that is essential, and often forgotten, in both running a business and developing a brand.*'

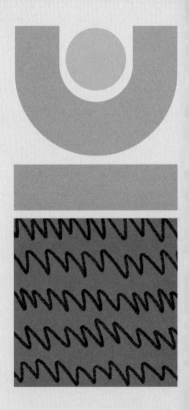

How do you describe the brand?

A PR stunt gone choco loco. We DIY'ed a chocolate bar, showed it's possible to make great-tasting chocolate without exploiting people, and disrupted the supermarket shelves with a unique, creative and bold yet positive and inviting brand.

What do you believe is the difference between running a business and being the custodian of a brand?

The person that runs a business should set the dot on the horizon, focus on the what. A brand developer focuses on the how, but both should equally ladder up to the why. Why does this company exist in the first place? It's this 'why' that is essential, and often forgotten, in both running a business and developing a brand. It's the question I ask most often, every day: Why? Like a professional two year old. Why do all chocolate bars look alike? Why are milk chocolate bars in the Netherlands blue, and dark chocolate red? And why oh why should we accept that the chocolate we enjoy is made with modern slavery and child labour? Always work from the why.

Tony's Chocolonely is changing the way chocolate is created, sold and consumed. Trying to shake up such a massive industry, with giants that have been utilising slave labour for decades, isn't an easy feat. How did you have the confidence to even start taking this on?

Tony's was born from investigative journalism, from a television program researching food production. After reading a small newspaper clipping about children being trafficked to cocoa plantations in West Africa, they decided to act. Suing big chocolate companies (Big Choco) was not an option, so Teun van de Keuken (or Tony, as he referred to himself internationally) decided to sue himself. He reasoned that if he kept eating chocolate, whilst knowing it was produced with modern slavery and child labour, he was guilty of maintaining just that. He ate twelve chocolate bars in front of witnesses and handed himself over to the authorities. He wasn't convicted, but the fire to battle this injustice was lit. Next up: his own bar. If no one was going to do it, f' it, we'll do it ourselves. And Tony's Chocolonely, Tony's lonely quest for fair, slave-free chocolate, was born.

So many people start out to build a brand that has impact but give up when it feels either too hard or beyond their skill or resource level. What have been some of the best tactics you employed at the start to move past these feelings?

To achieve our mission has always been our one and only objective, and that was and is the main driver shared by all Tonys. We exist to change the cocoa industry. To leave the world better than how we found it, not leave it richer. That makes our reason for being different than most other companies. This focus, and not being burdened by knowing how an industry works (which is a nice way of saying we didn't really know what we were doing), made us make radically different choices. We knew it could be done, and we are proving it can be. We see the impact we make, improving farmer's lives in Ghana and Côte d'Ivoire, and making incredibly tasty chocolate. That conviction has kept us going for nearly twenty years now.

Tony's brand values are so aligned with its actions, from website copy to recruitment practices and staff titles to professional development. It seems to live up to its brand purpose and mission at every touchpoint. How does this practically happen?

I'd love to say this is all on purpose and well managed, with clear guidelines and tools, but the truth is we're making it up as we go along. Tony's has grown organically, from an idea to a company, and allowed ourselves to make mistakes and learn from them. Now is actually the first time in eighteen years we're jotting down the brand guidelines properly in our Big, Red Blueprint. But it helps every Tony grow a strong sense of the brand, in which we invest time in the first weeks fresh Tonys join us. We have a Typical Tony's Time in which every aspect of the company is shared, with making your own bar, watching our documentary and talks from every team – also a Brand Camp on brand, design and marketing. Every Tony is connected in sharing the same mission, so everyone knows about the brand.

It's also vital we harbour the key marketing activities within the team. Our Creative Team, our Communications Team, Product Development and Digital – they are all in-house which ensures mostly everything will come from brand side and be on brand. I myself find it challenging to work with external creative agencies, as the brand is very nuanced and it takes a long time for people to get it. Externals often go crazy with the colours and visuals, but actually Tony's is very single-minded in colouring, and heavily copy focused. More often than not, it doesn't survive the purple cow check: if you can add a purple Milka cow to it and it fits, it's not Only Tony's. That's why I promote working together with external creatives, not having them work for us – we bring knowledge, consistency and experience on the brand, but we need them to get us out of that red bubble.

Tony's is one of few companies that has chosen to not only collaborate, but actively work, with its 'competitors' for the greater good with Tony's Open Chain. When and why did this happen and how can the brands of tomorrow take on this same collaborate-not-compete approach?
Our ambition is not to become the world's biggest chocolate company, if anything we would love to become obsolete! If we can change the industry and eradicate modern slavery and child labour from chocolate, we will gladly dissolve ourselves. To think from a mission-led starting point, to want to make an impact with every choice you make, forces you to think radically different. So when we see that our way of working, consisting of five basic sourcing principles, works, we don't want to keep it as our secret, slave-free recipe, we open it up for everyone to use! And

even more so, actively (sometimes forcibly) invite other players in the industry to join in.

What do you think the biggest myth is around the idea of building a brand today?
That it needs a big agency and a bigger bag of money to do so. I love it when a brand, especially a start-up brand, feels and looks like it's got real people behind it. I want to see the tape in the decor, talk to real people if I have a question. If I can believe a brand, believe it's real, I will be inclined to connect to their ideas – and maybe the product they're offering. It took me 10 minutes to come up with the design for our first red, milk chocolate bar. No brief, no budget, just that unpronounceable name and the size of the bar. No myths there!

What legacy would you like Tony's Chocolonely to leave behind?
It's very obvious, and I'm not just saying that because it's in my contract to do so, but it really is making an impact in West Africa. Changing the cocoa industry, an industry that has been a broken system for so long, is changing the world. Not sure if I'm going to be around to see it, but I would love it if we can, at some point, say we were part of that change. And, on a personal note, I'd love it if the wrapper design can survive as it is now and at some point someone will say: the person who made this really knew what they were doing. Even though I didn't, haha!

Tony's has proven that change can be achieved through committed brands. What advice would you give to someone reading this book who wants to focus more on people and the planet but feel they are too small to make a difference?
A phrase we used a lot when we kicked things off was one by Anita Roddick from The Body Shop: 'If you think you're too small to have an impact, try going to bed with a mosquito in the room.' Very true, and we've grown into that mosquito – and sometimes the elephant – in the bedroom. If you can truly change the life of one person, you've achieved so much already.

Why do you think building a brand, and not simply a business, is important today?

It first struck me we were building a brand, and not a business, when people in The Netherlands started referring to our bars as 'Tony's' and not 'chocolate bars'. A bar of Tony's became something different than a bar of chocolate. It was different, it was new, it was ... itself. People liked being seen with it. I remember seeing someone walk around with a Tony's T-shirt for the first time which I found remarkable; amazing that someone would associate themselves so much with a brand that they wear it on their body. So from the start, Tony's was a brand, even before it was a business. It was an idea, a conviction that became a company. And people pull towards ideas and things a brand represents, not the company itself.

Tony's gets a lot of fan mail, which I find amazing. Who sends messages to a brand they love? Especially in this day and age, when complaining and being offended seems to be the go-to way to interact with businesses. But people take the time to send us compliments, ideas for chocolate flavour combinations, birth cards of children called Tony, pictures of homemade wallpaper made from our wrappers ... everything! It's the brand that makes them do that.

Web: tonyschocolonely.com

IG: @tonyschocolonely_uk_ire

TT: @tonyschocolonely_uk_ire

Image: Tony's Chocolonely

04.

Where do you need to go?

When I was sixteen my father scheduled my very first driving lesson on our kitchen calendar. I can still recall my excitement at reading his small, wavy writing as I walked past the calendar every day. The first driving lesson is a huge moment for most teenagers and, with eighteen months to go until I could apply for my P-plater licence, I was keen to practise as much as I could. This was 1996, pre-internet and in a time when the public transport from the outer eastern suburb I lived in to the city was crappy, to say the least. Being able to drive represented freedom in my teenage mind and I had imagined myself cranking up the radio (yes, there wasn't even a CD player in the car at this stage) and driving my besties Vy and Lisa around town.

On the morning of my first driving lesson I was nervous and bursting to get into the car and out of the driveway. My father, sensing my excitement, relayed how important it was to be able to learn 'all the foundations' of driving. He reiterated, as he had done my whole life, what a privilege it was to have this freedom. My mother, who at the time knew exactly what was going to happen but gave nothing away, remarked while making her tea, 'Remember, a car can be a weapon in the wrong hands, always drive carefully.'

After what felt like hours, we finally got into the car; a light blue manual Holden Camira. My father went through the various buttons and switches, and we practised pushing the clutch down and switching gears. After a good 20 minutes I began to wonder when we might actually get going. Just as I thought Dad was getting himself set for my first go at driving, he asked me to unlock my seatbelt. What? This was not part of the plan. As he walked around in front of the car he called out to me, 'Okay, pop the lid up.' I did as he had just shown me a few minutes earlier. He gestured for me to get out, taught me how to secure the lid of the bonnet and then for the next two hours proceeded to teach me how to check the oil and water, clean and wipe the front windscreen, understand the elements of the engine and how to check the air pressure in a tyre. When we finished he smiled and said, 'Well, you did well for your first lesson, but there's one more tool you need to understand before you can get on the road.'

With frustration brewing and the realisation that my first driving lesson would not actually involve *driving*, I watched as he walked inside then came back out holding something behind his back. Beaming, he presented me with a brand-new *Melway* – a large A4-sized book that mapped, in detail, every single road, river, beach, roundabout and pathway in Victoria.

As we sat together on the front porch, he showed me how to navigate the maps while driving and to earmark the pages I would be using most often. I still remember our home address was page 49, reference E6. Much like the *A–Z* in London, the *Melway* became my go-to resource to track my journey, find out the best path or just to get curious about all the other parts of Victoria I might one day visit. Everything from birthday invitations and funeral booklets, through to coffee stains and an assortment of bookmarks would be left within the pages of my *Melway*. While it may feel incredibly old-school, I loved the freedom that the *Melway* represented – I could simply choose a path and follow it all the way to my destination.

In the same way that the *Melway* offered different paths to the same destination, depending on whether you wanted the scenic route or a faster concrete freeway, the road to building a brand can also look different for different people.

Where do you need to go?

When I began my own journey in brand building, I was just twenty-one and working as an executive assistant in a very small advertising agency, deep in the East End of London. My then boss was fond of telling me about the 3C model when it came to building a brand: customer, cost and competition. I still recall his Northern accent as he drummed into me the importance of all three Cs when coming up with strategies and tactics.

As my career developed and I moved into my first full-time role in Australia, as an editor for street press and custom publishing titles, I was schooled in another model, the brand as authority. These were the heady days of journalism before social media stole the advertising dollars that made our publications thick and our founders rich. As editor for the first custom publishing title for David Jones (one of two major department stores in Australia), I was charged with helping the brand tap into a new, younger, edgier and more fashion-conscious consumer through marketing and content. This new consumer not only cared about how the fashion labels looked, but also who was behind them. It was about bringing a more human element into branding and the opportunity for connection with topics that were not purely concerned with the product itself. The brand was seen in a more holistic way and its founders were the influencers that people wanted to know about – sometimes even more so than the products they sold.

While working for Pearson (one of the largest publishing companies in the world), I learned about the importance of innovation in brand. This was a time when interactive whiteboards were beginning to be utilised in classrooms across the globe. Educational resources that to date had largely been print-based (think textbooks and worksheets) had to transform into digital tools that could still be as engaging and carefully created to keep the brand and its products relevant. In addition, I was working on a project to sell Western educational tools into a Middle-Eastern market and so questions of 'What makes a global brand?' were raised, along with 'How can our products be more inclusive so that they are more easily adaptable for other territories?' It was a time of growth and change for the brand with respect to its long-term vision and standing in the global marketplace.

When I branched out on my own and started a brand content business in 2007, I worked with numerous founders of retail and fashion brands, helping them take their first tentative steps into the world of online and eCommerce. At the same time (and to stabilise my business income), I wrote a weekly column for *The Age* newspaper (one of two main newspapers in Melbourne) where I would relay the latest brand launches, collections and events. I would also ghostwrite books for celebrities, helping them to build their brand authority and awareness in various sectors. This period was much aligned with the brand model of the 3Ps – personality, purpose and promise. It was all about the people behind a brand, what their purpose was and the promise they hoped to deliver on through their products, services and overall experience.

Years later, when I moved back to London I worked at Open University on its MBA program, trying to find the best ways to engage an audience that was predominately made up of students learning while also working a full-time job. The content not only had to be engaging and impact-driven, cultivating a community when no one had actually met in person, but also accessible to people living with a range of disabilities. This role taught me the power of being inclusive and the need to consider your audience at every possible touchpoint. The brand had to live up to the promise of being an 'open' place of learning.

Business *to* Brand

Shortly thereafter, I began working at Amazon in the UK, where building the brand was all about alignment with key values – in Amazon's case, convenience was the number one value. I remember a mentor telling me that 'so long as you can prove the convenience of the customer is at the forefront of your decisions and you have analytics to back up your ideas, you will be supported in making a change'. When I moved to Audible UK and later consulted to Audible AU, I was schooled in future thinking and the power of retention and building brand loyalty. Audible is a brand that relies entirely on retention, on people wanting to stay loyal month after month, year after year, and on people choosing to indulge in their love of books in a new way (through the medium of audio). At the time (in 2012) audiobooks were still seen as something only enjoyed by the elderly or those with impaired vision. Podcasts were still in their infancy and so many of our conversations internally were about how to shift perspectives, change people's behaviour and get our brand to be at the centre of people's everyday routines. The greatest competitor at the time was Amazon's Kindle. People had been able to move from a physical book to a digital one, and we were trying to get them to change their behaviour again and move from a digital reader to an audiobook. This was really all about creating a brand that fit with their busy lifestyle and enabled them to indulge in books while also keeping fit, cooking, driving or gardening.

At a digital agency back home in Melbourne, I headed up the Audience Engagement arm, looking at ways brands could begin to utilise online content and new ways of marketing to better engage and grow their audiences. I would hold brand content workshops, consulting with companies as established as Porsche and as emerging as Scrunch, on how to get their brand messages across while also leaving room for interaction and customer engagement. How do you create brand content that speaks to your objectives as a business while cultivating a community to form around the brand? How do you create so much value in what you're putting out that people not only want to be part of your community but also actively engage others to be part of it too? These were some of the key questions I would work to answer for clients in this role.

The education continued when I moved into another brand role and eventually became Head of Marketing at MIMCO (a large accessories retail brand). At first my role was largely focused on how to create internal systems and ways of working that would enable all departments (e.g. design, retail, digital, PR, visual merchandising) to gift their knowledge to the whole company, to create the most consistent brand content and marketing experiences, whether someone was shopping in-store, speaking to a customer service representative on the phone, emailing the eCommerce team or browsing the products via social media. It was about consistency of brand across all touchpoints and a review of the key messages and promises. This was only a decade ago, and yet in Australia much of the retail landscape at the time was still dominated by the use of white models in all brand collateral. MIMCO was one of the few big retailers who chose to do things differently by using models from all backgrounds for campaigns and online catalogues, as well as showcasing its products, such as scarves, in a variety of uses from neck scarves to head wraps to hijabs. Instagram had just launched a few years earlier and MIMCO was again at the forefront of merging social media and eCommerce through the use of user-generated content (UGC) being transferred from a MIMCO fan's Instagram page straight to product detail pages, which led to higher conversion (vs pages that only used model shots to show the product) and the need for more 'real' content to be created.

Where do you need to go?

This was a time when brand transparency was becoming more important than ever before. Whether it was a collaboration with the United Nations Ethical Fashion Initiative or a keynote from our Managing and Creative Director at the time, the audience expected (quite rightly) full transparency from MIMCO and from all the brands they engaged with. This time in my career really taught me about the power of audience, the need for honest communication and the importance of analytical data to truly survey the brand landscape. It was about tuning into what the customer was telling us (both actively and passively) and engaging with them in a way that felt genuine. It was also a time when all companies were being forced to pull back the curtain and show the behind-the-scenes from what goes into a campaign shoot through to what goes into the making of each product.

Since beginning my own business at the tail end of 2015, I have had the privilege of working with thousands of companies, many of which are recognised and respected creative brands. I have been able to witness what works and what doesn't when it comes to creating a meaningful brand that not only fulfils, and often exceeds, the expectations of its audiences but also fulfils – financially and emotionally – the needs of its founder/s and staff. I have seen a plethora of brand style guides, DNAs, focus group pathways and brand strategy bibles. I have seen what works and what doesn't and I have been able to separate the fluff from the foundations that set a brand up for success.

All of this is to say that there is not one perfect way to build a brand – a quick Google search will show you an entire alphabet of 'brand models', from the 4Cs and the 3Ps to the 5Ss, 6As and the 3Rs. It can be confusing and overwhelming, but remember – just like using the *Melway* – you may well take a slightly different path to the brand owner next to you to reach a similar destination.

To simplify things and remove the overwhelm, you will find here the most important elements of a brand that I believe you must work through, understand, define and nurture, if you want to create a brand that has meaning for its existence at its core.

These are the elements that I have found consistently work to transform a business into a brand, regardless of its size or age. These are the elements that could be applied in every company I have ever been employed by and every single business I have worked with as a coach, mentor and teacher.

Business *to* Brand

In Chapter 2 you learned about each of these elements (remember my ACE brand model?). You can see the full list of elements in Figure 2.1 (page 28).

Now, let's look at each of the elements in A (Authenticity), C (Creativity) and E (Elevation) again. For A and C you'll find examples of existing brands that exemplify each particular element. This is a little harder to do for E as much of this work is done behind the scenes.

(A disclaimer before we jump in: brands are an ever-evolving entity and, much like humans, they can and often do make mistakes. While I am highlighting one brand element that these particular companies do well at this particular moment in time, that is not to say they are flawless in every other area of their business or that in the future this element of their brand won't change.)

AREA: AUTHENTICITY		
ELEMENT	**ASK**	**EXAMPLE BRAND**
Purpose	What is the deepest reason for your business's existence?	Who Gives a Crap: The Aussie start-up has become a recognised brand worldwide. A huge part of this is down to its simple purpose – to utilise a product we use daily to change the lives of others. In short: give a crap. whogivesacrap.org
Vision	Where are you going? This is your answer to: how are you changing the world?	Warby Parker: On the surface Warby Parker creates beautiful eyewear. On a deeper level the company's greater vision (#BoomTish) is to help people impacted by a lack of access to eye health and quality reading programs. warbyparker.com
Mission	What are you doing right now? What are you doing that is meaningful?	Patagonia: Since its start, the brand has been all about helping people explore the world around them while trying to reduce their impact on it. Its mission statement sums this up: 'Build the best product, cause no unnecessary harm, use business to inspire and implement solutions to the environmental crisis.' patagonia.com

Where do you need to go?

AREA: AUTHENTICITY		
ELEMENT	**ASK**	**EXAMPLE BRAND**
Values and beliefs	What are the guiding values and beliefs that underpin the brand? Are they aligned both externally (i.e. customer-facing) and internally (i.e. do your staff feel aligned with them)?	Mustard: This global brand aligns its content and values across all touchpoints. For example, one of its key values is Honesty. During COVID-19 the cost of steel skyrocketed which led Mustard to increase its prices. At its earliest opportunity it shared this with its customers alongside graphics showing the increase and how it was impacting the business. mustardmade.com
Creations	What are you creating? How do your products and services change the lives of those who interact and engage with them?	Glossier: This US-based beauty brand is one of the most recognised when it comes to innovation and listening to its audience's needs. New products are often created after deep consultation with its audience – from influential #MUAs (makeup artists) through to the everyday person who buys products online. glossier.com
Audience	Who most needs what your brand delivers? How does your brand speak to their desires, alleviate their pain points and help them overcome their fears?	Walker and Company: With a tagline that simply states: 'Our purpose is to make health and beauty simple for people of colour', this company knows exactly who its audience is and how to ensure it is tailoring every product, every launch and every single brand campaign to directly speak to, attract and nurture its chosen audience. walkerandcompany.com

Business *to* Brand

AREA: CREATIVITY		
ELEMENT	**ASK**	**EXAMPLE BRAND**
Positioning	What position do you want your brand to have in the minds of your ideal consumer?	Tesla: Regardless of your thoughts on Elon Musk, Tesla has cemented itself as the go-to brand in the automotive industry for its first-in-market approach to electric cars. Regardless of other brands available, when people see a Tesla they are reminded of the link between electric cars and the environment, which Tesla has worked hard to cultivate. tesla.com
Competition	Why would someone choose your brand to stay loyal to when there are others in the market?	Squarespace: Unlike many of its competitors, Squarespace has an incredibly simple and intuitive drag-and-drop method for people looking to design and update their own website. It is not built for web developers but for the everyday small business owner who wants a website that looks good and is easy to maintain. squarespace.com
Name and story	How does your name, and your storytelling, allow for change, growth and elevation of your brand?	Monday: Previously named daPulse, Monday rebranded with a name that aligns with what the brand offers: project management software and a way of organising business tasks. Many people start their work week on a Monday and this is when many team meetings will happen and goals for the next week will be set. The name works well with the overall brand message. monday.com

Where do you need to go?

AREA: CREATIVITY		
ELEMENT	**ASK**	**EXAMPLE BRAND**
Personality and voice	How does your brand's personality and voice help it connect, nurture and keep people loyal?	Sage x Clare: This much-loved Australian lifestyle brand is instantly recognisable and it sets itself apart from other brands within the homeware and lifestyle sector through its beautiful, lighthearted and joyful take on design, perfectly articulated via its tone of voice. sageandclare.com
Visual identity	How do you use visual language to get your key brand messages across?	Apple: Apple is so adored that people will even keep the packaging of a product, long after it is required. Why? Because it looks so good. With minimal, clean and sleek designs and quality materials, the Apple packaging adds to the entire brand experience. apple.com
Content	Which themes or pillars are you known for creating valuable content around, and how can you utilise these to cement your place in the minds of your audience?	Later: This social media scheduling tool is known for creating valuable content that's useful whether you are a paid member or just searching for updated information about how to use your social platforms more effectively. From annual calendars full of key national days through to updates on the latest social tools, it helps the brand remain front of mind for anyone working in social. later.com

Business *to* Brand

AREA: ELEVATION	
ELEMENT	**ASK**
Connection channels	How can you utilise these channels to help guide people through an incredible experience with your brand, from initial awareness to becoming an advocate?
People	How do you ensure you hire, nurture and retain staff who absolutely love the brand and become its greatest ambassadors?
Authority building	What are you the go-to brand for and how do you keep this reputation going year after year?
Future thinking	How are you staying informed about, and ahead of, the changes that will impact your audience and your business?
Analytics and impact	Which analytics will form the basis of your decisions as a brand? How do you create the systems to support this knowledge at every touchpoint?
Alignment	How aligned is your brand with the promise you're giving to your audience/s?

Now that you have considered the ACE brand elements in relation to brands and companies you may not only know but have also been a customer of (or even an ambassador for!), it's time to revisit the benchmark matrix you completed in Chapter 3 (page 62).

Knowing what you know now, consider where you would like to end up by the time you finish working through this book. Reading through the previous examples of brands might well have allowed you to conjure up ideas for your own brand elements and perhaps (hopefully) enabled you to see that it's not as difficult as you might have imagined.

Use the table in Figure 4.1 on the opposite page to set yourself a future benchmark against each of the ACE brand elements. You can review this at the end of this book and see how the results compare. Use the same scoring system as outlined on page 61.

Where do you need to go?

Figure 4.1 **Benchmarks for your ACE brand by the end of this book**

AREA	ELEMENT	1	2	3	4	5	6
A (Authenticity)	Purpose						
	Vision						
	Mission						
	Values and beliefs						
	Creations						
C (Creativity)	Positioning						
	Competition						
	Name and story						
	Personality and voice						
	Visual identity						
	Content						
E (Elevation)	Connection channels						
	People						
	Authority building						
	Future thinking						
	Analytics and impact						
	Alignment						

Business *to* Brand

How did that feel? Scary? Exciting? Either way you now have an objective to work towards as you continue your journey of building a brand you love.

But *how* will you make this happen?

As you may have guessed by now, I'm a big fan of quotes (yep, happy to admit it #QuotesForever). When I was seventeen and in my first year of university, I went to visit my uncle Cecil, who was then living in New Orleans, Louisiana. As we chatted about my education and my workload, my uncle remarked: 'Remember, if you fail to plan, you plan to fail.'

These words (I believe made famous by Benjamin Franklin) have stayed with me ever since. While I don't believe you automatically fail without a plan, I do believe a good plan breaks down what can feel like an overwhelming task into manageable pieces that are easier to mentally absorb.

The next few chapters of this book will ask you to get into the details of building your brand and doing the work required to create a more meaningful entity. From going deep into your big vision to dissecting the best systems to support your sustainability as a business, you'll have to do the work to see the results.

Consider a timeline for working through all of the elements in the ACE brand model. As there are eighteen elements you may decide to map out a certain amount of time each week over the next eighteen weeks. Or you may decide you want to devote one month to each of the areas (authenticity, creativity and elevation) and get this done within the next three months. Whatever you decide, consider a basic plan for actioning this. (You can find a free twelve-month calendar template to help plan this out at mydailybusiness.com/freestuff – and also at Figure 8.3 on page 204.)

Scheduling this time now may feel tedious but it is going to help you in the long run. As you're doing this it may be helpful to reflect on something else you initially viewed as overwhelming but have now accomplished, whether that is finishing your studies, having a child or ticking off a fitness goal. Chances are you started all of those journeys with small steps that, when you look back, created momentum and helped you achieve your goal. This is no different.

Consider this planning the first of many steps you will take in your brand journey.

Where do you need to go?

TASKS TO CONSIDER

Just as no two businesses are exactly the same, the journey to creating a brand will be different for you compared to another brand founder.

Utilising the knowledge you have gained so far, work through the following questions or download them in a worksheet form online via the QR code below.

1. *Which brand models have you heard of? If you have worked through some before, what did you feel was lacking and what were the best parts?*

2. *When reviewing the elements of an ACE brand and the examples of existing brands, which stood out most to you? Why do you think this is? Do you perhaps see your own brand in that example brand?*

3. *Think about the journeys you have taken so far in your life (e.g. becoming a parent, getting married, getting an education or starting a business). Was the journey straightforward for you? Why/Why not? How did you cut yourself some slack and how might you remind yourself of that experience as you work through the rest of this book and your brand journey?*

4. *Set your future benchmarks in Figure 4.1 (page 83).*

5. *Consider any obstacles that may hinder your schedule for completion of this book. How might you get on the front foot of these now (e.g. rearranging commitments or informing people that you're unavailable during these times)?*

6. *Go back to your answers from Chapter 1 where you listed some of the brands you love. Keeping in mind the eighteen elements of an ACE brand, how many of those elements do these brands do well?*

Before we jump into Chapter 5 and learn how you can build an authentic foundation for your brand, we will hear from Laura Thompson, who with Sarah Sheridan founded Clothing The Gaps, a lifestyle and apparel brand that has become synonymous with creating merch with a meaning.

Scan for digital worksheet

Image: Maria Palacios (pollypalacios.myportfolio.com)

Profile:
Clothing The Gaps

What originally started as an Aboriginal health promotion and community engagement company has become one of the most impactful lifestyle and clothing brands to come out of Australia. Clothing The Gaps sparks conversation, collaboration and community around the history, challenges and celebrations of First Nations people and, in turn, of all Australians. Co-founder and Gunditjmara woman Laura Thompson talks us through the brand that is Clothing The Gaps.

How would you describe the brand?

I find myself always relaying our taglines because they are the truth of what we do. We unite Aboriginal people through fashion, create merch with a message and we encourage people to wear their values. What I love the most about the business is that we have Mob in our heart and everyone else in mind.

The name of the business is a play on 'Closing the Gap' [an Australian government framework that aims to reduce the gaps between Aboriginal and Torres Strait Islander peoples and non-Indigenous Australians on key health, education and economic opportunity targets]. When you visit our shop, you're entering a culturally safe Blak space. You will be welcomed by First Nations retail staff who display their Mob/tribe connections on their name tags. The cool thing is that if you nail and create safe environments for First Nations people, you nail it for everyone.

At the core of what we do is centre First Nations people in our product, in our messaging and in our business model. We have a Mob-Only range, which has messages that are personal and only relevant to Aboriginal and Torres Strait Islander people. This is a unique offering that's part of the bigger picture of how we continue to nurture, elevate and celebrate First Nations people in the business.

We also offer a 15% Mob discount. When you purchase from us, our retail staff will ask (and they do it so beautifully): 'Do you identify as Aboriginal or Torres Strait Islander? We offer a discount for Mob, does that apply to you?' The customer will say yes or no and then that's it. We have brought price equity into the business. I don't know of any other brand that does this, so I'm proud of that. We have to remember that our business exists because of the success and struggle of Aboriginal people and we see price equity as something small we can do to take care of Mob.

What do you think is the difference between running a business vs. being the custodian of a brand?

Clothing The Gaps is a baby of ours that [co-founder] Sarah Sheridan (who is non-Indigenous) and I are growing together. The intensity, care and love that we put in is endless. If we were just selling T-shirts, we wouldn't be able to maintain the intensity. The T-shirts were always a vehicle for starting a conversation to address First Nations justice. It was also a vehicle to be able to fund our Clothing The Gaps Foundation (a not-for-profit health promotion organisation) that aims to add years to Aboriginal peoples' lives.

We are not businesspeople; both Sarah and I have a preventative health background. We're public health professionals. I have a Masters in Public Health, so we really knew nothing about fashion, retail and business when we started.

What we do know about is community, how to bring communities together and how to create behaviour change, which is really what you do in health promotion. We're great at that. When it comes to selling a T-shirt, what we're selling is messaging to get people to spark conversations in their personal and professional circles that supports truth telling, social and political change and better outcomes for First Nations people and communities. We sell a lot of T-shirts to non-Indigenous people, which makes sense. Mob are only 3% of the population. So a stack of our supporters are people who care about Aboriginal and Torres Strait Islander people. They were just waiting for an actual invitation and opportunity to start having these conversations, and we do that through clothing.

Did you consider it a brand when you started? What were some key milestones in realising you had built a brand?

No. When we started originally, it was about creating merchandise for an Aboriginal health promotion company called Spark Health that Sarah and I had formed together (we had previously worked together at Victorian Aboriginal Health Service). We used that merch to encourage Aboriginal people to participate in a health program. If you came to four of the six sessions, you got some merch. People came for the shirt but ended up becoming a part of a community.

You create a sense of community among people by wearing the same clothes, just like a team. The clothes that were created for the health programs had Aboriginal designs on them and they reinforced cultural identity. At that point in time, there weren't a whole lot of retailers creating clothes that made you feel proud to be Aboriginal, or to support Mob. We called the original brand 'Spark Merch', which was a terrible name!

There was a moment when someone asked, 'Can I wear this as a non-Indigenous person?' and I would have an exhausting conversation to explain the positive flow on effects that wearing the T-shirts would have for First Nations communities. Then it hit us. We are 'clothing' the gap and I could save a whole lot of energy and yarns by simply communicating our purpose if we changed the brand name. That was a game changer. People knew about 'Closing the Gap' so we began saying, 'You can help us close the gap by you *clothing* the gap'. When we first started we did promote the brand to non-Indigenous people to let them know that it was okay. We want you to buy into the brand. This is an invitation for you.

The other big branding decision besides the name was when we started to label products as 'Ally Friendly' or 'Mob Only'. In that shift, we saw an increase in profitability because it made shopping with us easier for non-Indigenous people. It instantly answered the question of 'Can I wear that? Is it cultural appropriation?' It gave people confidence in purchasing. But people need to remember that 'ally' isn't a noun, it's a verb. It's a way of being. You can't just buy a T-shirt and be done. You need to do the work too.

There were also key points in our brand journey with two massive copyright issues (first with American clothing company The Gap, and then with a non-Indigenous clothing company over copyright restrictions surrounding the depiction of the Aboriginal flag on our products). These stressful times gave us a whole lot of organic media traffic. In some ways, it's been hard but we have been a brand that's been featured a lot for our advocacy in the mainstream media.

COVID-19 also had a huge impact on our ability to deliver Community health programs, so we made the decision to lean right in to growing the brand. It absolutely took off!

How do you measure your impact as a brand?

We have a pretty small team here. Measuring our impact is something we almost don't have time for because we're too busy in the 'doing'. That's why the accreditations from Supply Nation, B-Corp, Social Traders and Ethical Clothing Australia are important for us. It gives our customer a level of security knowing that someone else is certifying us. They're checking that what we claim is true.

I also signed up to Indigenous Art Code when we did our first collab with a First Nations artist. I was like, 'Sign me up. I want to know if I'm doing things the right way from the beginning.' Lots of people talk about B-Corp being a hard certification to get, but because we got it so early and we're already values-led, we weren't retrofitting what we were doing. We are, from the get-go, making the best choices around our people, community, sustainability and environment.

Profit, for us, has been our lowest priority. It's something we haven't focused on and that's probably because of the Aboriginal Community sector we come from and from not being businesspeople.

Clothing The Gaps is so much more than a clothing lifestyle brand. Your items are there as conversation starters for First Nations people and allies alike. How do you enable so many impactful and change-making conversations from a simple T-shirt?

The T-shirts, in and of themselves, allow people to influence their circles. I'd sometimes find myself making resources for the website and think, 'Who am I educating? Why am I writing this blog on why January 26th is not a date to celebrate? If the brand is centering Mob, why am I writing this?' It became clear that we're helping to reduce the burden for Mob so they don't have to keep explaining the same thing all the time. They can just send a link whenever someone asks them the question. We want to share the burden and the responsibility with non-Indigenous people to carry those conversations in their spaces.

When you buy a T-shirt from us, you get a great T-shirt but it also comes with responsibility and an expectation of continued action. The Free The Flag campaign was a perfect example of this. We asked people who bought a T-shirt to talk about the issue with their community, sign the petition, and use an email template to write to their local minister. When the [Aboriginal] flag was freed years later, the federal minister for Indigenous Australians, Ken Wyatt, said he couldn't ignore the number of emails he was getting on the issue. It was people power.

I never call people who buy from us 'customers', I hate that word. It's too transactional and they're not just buying a tee, they're doing other things as well. We call them our Clothing The Gaps fam, they're supporters of social change. What we've built is a community base of people who want to make this world, or Australia, a better place for First Nations people; buying a tee is part of the action.

In health promotion you're often getting people to change behaviours and I'd often think, 'How do I create a message that people can remember for a more complex issue that requires that person to then take action?' We approach Clothing The Gaps with the same mindset and practice. We are good at communicating complex problems and issues that Aboriginal people face in clear and memorable ways. We know that a lot of people are not reading detailed documents and are getting their news in bites on social media so we aim to simplify the content to hook them in, and then encourage them to dig deeper.

Why do you think building a brand and not just a business is important today?

For me, it's simply about the brand's ability to influence and create social change, and self-determine futures. I heard once that brands are more influential than politicians – I believe it! Bigger brands certainly have bigger social media followings than pollies. Wearing our Clothing The Gaps merch allows us to talk without talking. We are changing the way spaces look and feel one tee at a time – we are creating walking billboards. Our T-shirts allow us to go into a space and say 'This is me. This is what I care about and all Australians should be celebrating and respecting the 65,000 years of culture in this land.

Whilst it might not be everyone's culture, it's the foundation of Australia's history. This country has the oldest continuous living culture, and we should all be proud of it.

We're a merch with a message.

Web: clothingthegaps.com.au

IG: @clothingthegaps

TT: @clothing_the_gaps

05.

Start with authenticity

A few years ago, my husband and I embarked on the task of renovating our little log cabin home in North Warrandyte, a bushy green-wedge suburb on the outskirts of Melbourne. We had purchased the home seven years earlier, wide-eyed and excited about the 'work' we could do over the years to make it absolutely perfect.

We were young, inexperienced and excited to be owning (or renting from the bank!) our first home.

Over time we fixed things as and when we could afford them, put in some skylights to brighten things up and changed the outdated lighting to something more modern. We invested in insulation to reduce heating costs and linked up the water tank. More often, we fixed things when they were absolutely necessary – think an overly priced new hot water system, windows that were cracked in hailstorms and (the most fun!) a new sewerage connection.

As the years passed and our little family grew from two adults, one toddler and one dog, to two adults, one pre-teen, one toddler and two dogs, we saw the need to either move or make the house larger. After two years of searching (a period which incorporated massive housing price hikes and the world's longest lockdowns #LoveYouMelbourne) we made the decision to renovate. After all, we figured we could then really decide what we wanted and make it the perfect home for our family.

Meeting with recommended architects, we were excited about everything that was possible. The dream kitchen renovation, the wide and winding spiral staircase I'd always imagined, a Japanese bath within a rejuvenating and spacious bathroom, a large open lounge room gushing with natural sunlight that entered via a wall of windows, and a wide deck that would fully envelop the whole house. It was stunning and would create the sanctuary we had always imagined coming home to. We talked to our children about what we envisioned, excitedly got to work on various Pinterest boards (an outdoor fully rocked swimming pool? Why not? A deep walk-in-wardrobe? Sure!) and downloaded tiny line drawings of armchairs and circular tables to mock up our vision.

As our (read: my) wants and desires spiralled, so too did the list of experts we needed to visit our home and assess … well, everything. From a range of strategists to determine the best approach for the local council, through to numerous bushfire experts to assess the danger levels of our precise location, through to soil testers, multiple surveyors, engineers and town-planning experts, the list seemed endless.

As much as I had hoped to get started on the designs and see our 'dream home' come to life, the groundwork had to be laid to figure out what was even possible. Rather than racing ahead to the visuals and imagery I wanted to see created, there were endless Zoom meetings about specs and regulations, legal ramifications, and ethical and environmental considerations. Instead of choosing colour swatches and sorting through tile samples, we were looking at Excel files to assess if the bushfire regulations meant we could afford another two centimetres of a living room, and choosing between non-dyed grey or painted black non-combustible concrete sheets. Eighteen months passed without a final design and while it was frustrating, it also showcased the importance of doing the groundwork first. Better to identify a problem when still in the design stages than when we were building and couldn't make any changes.

Start with authenticity

This experience mirrors branding and rebranding for so many small business owners. The seemingly fun, sexy and exciting part – choosing colour palettes and a typeface, designing the homepage of the website and coming up with a shot list for your brand photoshoot – can't happen until the other crucial and foundational work has been done. Sometimes this work can seem tedious, but when it comes to building a brand and not just a business, it is absolutely essential.

You cannot create a brand without laying the foundation and the biggest element of that foundation needs to be *authenticity*. It is from your authentic core that everything else in your brand will result – from your offerings and revenue streams through to the way you hire, retain and nurture staff. Authenticity is absolutely crucial for a brand to not only flourish in alignment with its values, vision and beliefs, but also for it to build and retain trust with those who encounter it.

One of the quickest ways to lose trust in a brand is to sense that it is inauthentic – that who it purports to be and the values and beliefs that guide it are nothing more than words on a page or a trending topic on social media. We have all encountered brands that proclaim to be something they are not, brands that shout loudly on social platforms about their commitment to diversity while still employing an all-white workforce, brands that greenwash their marketing while having next to no transparency over their supply chains, brands that claim to be providing health benefits for the masses while utilising child labour to fatten up their margins.

When someone starts a business with the hope of building a brand but does little to interrogate and investigate their practices in relation to the authenticity of their messaging, purpose and operations, they will fail. A well-designed logo can only get you so far. Understanding the importance of genuine authenticity and how it shows up in your brand today, tomorrow and forever is imperative to any long-term success.

Authenticity in a brand can show up in a plethora of forms (just as inauthenticity can). Within the ACE brand model, laying the foundation of a genuinely authentic brand includes understanding and aligning to your brand's:

- purpose
- vision
- mission
- values and beliefs
- creations
- audience.

On the following pages you will find practices, frameworks and tasks that will help you dive into each of these six components.

Remember, authenticity is not something you can conjure up over the course of a weekend. It is a metric by which you will and should be judged for the entirety of your brand's existence. While these tasks will help you cement the foundations of brand authenticity, they should never become a 'set and forget' strategy that you fail to assess, adhere to and audit with every future brand decision.

Let's begin.

Authenticity: Purpose

The very core of your brand and the reason so many of us begin businesses is for a purpose greater than simply financial gain. It is the catalyst that helps inspire yourself as the leader within your company, your staff and anyone working within it, as well as those who choose to allow your brand into their lives. When a brand's purpose is clear and meaningful, it helps cultivate a community within and around it who believe in and champion its success. Your purpose is the reason behind the entire business or brand idea igniting. It fuels your origin story and continues to light up the direction the brand will take today, tomorrow and into the future.

For some of you reading this, the term 'purpose' may feel somewhat diluted due in large part to its overuse by inauthentic brands that are quick to shout about purpose but slow – if not entirely unable – to align with it. If this is you, I would ask you to consider granting it back the power it deserves and spending the time necessary to uncover your own brand purpose. Remember, it has to feel authentic, clear and able to be easily relayed.

To do this, it may be helpful to spend time considering your answers to the following questions:

- Why did the brand begin?

- What is its origin story?

- What was the catalyst to move from an idea to an entity?

- Why, apart from money, is the brand in existence?

- What felt important about bringing this brand to life?

- Why does it matter?

- Who benefits from it? (Who does/will the brand serve?)

- How is it unique? (Are you creating an experience like no other brand in its industry? Are you solving a problem that hasn't been addressed up to this point?)

- What is your motivation?

These are just some of the questions that may help you define your purpose – the overarching reason behind your brand's existence.

In Chapter 3, I outlined some future-thinking exercises that may help you to define your own brand purpose. If you haven't already, revisit these exercises on page 54.

Once you have some thoughts written down, you can begin to cull and get to the heart of your brand purpose – that is to craft a brand purpose that is strong, succinct and easily understood. It may help to enter what you've written down into a word cloud tool and see which words and phrases are the most used. It may also help to get creative and draw your purpose then look at which colours, icons and symbols you have chosen to visually represent it. Or it may be worth spending some time reflecting on how your purpose might be portrayed in a film scene or choice of song.

Regardless, you want to reflect on how this brand purpose can and will be communicated.

Most brands opt for a purpose statement, which is usually a one to two sentence statement that relays the purpose to anyone who comes into contact with the brand.

Some examples of this are:

- Bodyform: We break V-Zone taboos to free women from stigma.

- Charles Schwab: To champion every client's goals with passion and integrity.

- eBay: To empower people and create economic opportunity for all.

Have a go at crafting your own purpose statement. Taking your answers to the questions above, what could you summarise in one to two sentences? Have a go at using this to craft your own purpose statement. You may wish to utilise AI tools to help with initial ideas for this. This may take you minutes (especially if you already have one you're happy with) or it may take weeks. Either way it should be in alignment with your genuine reason for being and feel 100% authentic to you and your customers.

When you're ready, let's talk vision.

Authenticity: Vision

The next thing to get super clear on when it comes to creating an authentic base for your ACE brand is to define the vision.

Now, you may be an established business owner wanting to change things up and cement your company as a brand. In this case, you may have started your business with a vision statement that just doesn't seem to fit anymore. Or perhaps you are just getting started with your business and have plenty of ideas for its vision but are finding it difficult to define.

I like to think of the vision of a business as a torch that can shine a light into the best possible future for your brand. The vision is what keeps you centred, grounded and focused on the future. It's the 'true north' that keeps you focused on what it is you're trying to build and why it's so important. If you had to define it in one simple icon, it would be a picture of the globe, signalling the impact your brand has on the world at large.

You may be wondering how this differs to your purpose. While your purpose is the battery within that torch, the vision provides the light, even in the darkest of situations when things may falter, when customers and clients are lacking in abundance and when stress is ever present. To put it simply, you can think of your vision as your biggest, boldest goal and your purpose as the motivation or fuel that powers it.

Much like a purpose statement, a brand's vision can be delivered via a vision statement that is often only a sentence or two, and it should be clear enough that anyone outside the brand can understand it. It can also be brought to life via a manifesto, song or mini movie. If you'd rather try something a little more left of centre, go right ahead.

Here are some brand examples to help you consider what your own brand vision statement might look like:

- Apple: To make the best products on earth and to leave the world better than we found it.

- Oxfam: A world without poverty.

- Dove: We are here to help women everywhere develop a positive relationship with the way they look, helping them raise their self-esteem and realise their full potential.

To define your own vision statement, consider your answers to the following questions:

- What is the biggest, boldest goal you have as a business?

- What does the brand look like ten or even twenty years from now?

- What is the greatest dream your business could realise?

- What is the greatest impact your business could have on the world?

Your answers should be concise and easily understood by anyone working within or associated with your brand, as well as clearly define what impact you'll have in the long term.

It is crucial to remember that your vision statement is a living document that should be reviewed, analysed and adhered to when making any decision for the brand.

Let's move on to your mission.

Authenticity: Mission

The third element in building authenticity is understanding – and staying aligned with – your brand mission.

Now, out of ALL of the brand elements, I think mission and vision are often misunderstood, either as one and the same thing (they are not) or that one is more important than the other (again, I would disagree with this line of thinking).

Where your vision is your future focus and BIG-picture goal, your mission defines what you're doing right here, right now (did you hear Fatboy Slim singing those last four words? Just me?). It is all the things you are doing in the current state, whereas your vision is the things you will achieve in the (desired) future state.

A brand's mission encompasses its audience and its objectives, and outlines how it will reach both. Much like a purpose and vision statement, your mission can also be conveyed in a one to two-line line statement, or perhaps even a whole paragraph. Again, it's not about ticking a box. It's about crafting a mission statement that feels in alignment with your brand, your purpose and your audience (an area we will get into shortly). If you want to communicate your mission as a poem, go right ahead. So long as it's clear and able to be expressed easily to others.

You may wish to work through these questions to help you uncover and craft your mission statement:

- Who is your brand for?

- Why do they love it?

- What does it do for them?

- How does it do this?

- What does it do to achieve your objectives?

- How does it do this?

- What does your business sell?

- Why is it not just different, but better than others in the market?

- What is the image you are trying to create with your brand?

- Why does anyone care?

Once you have written down some thoughts, cull anything unnecessary until you're left with a succinct, easily understood statement. Again, you may wish to use AI tools or, if you have the resources, a copywriter to help you with this.

Here are some examples of other brands' mission statements:

- Who Gives a Crap: We donate 50% of our profits to ensure everyone has access to clean water and a toilet within our lifetime.

- MoMA: We aspire to be a catalyst for experimentation, learning and creativity, a gathering place for all, and a home for artists and their ideas.

- Google: To organise the world's information and make it universally accessible and useful.

What is your mission statement? Spend some time crafting yours and remember it's better to have something that you can tweak and assess vs a blank page. Don't let perfection get in the way of making a start.

When you have your mission statement, you may wish to get buy-in from everyone else in the company and possibly test it with key clients and customers.

It's also at this stage – once clear on your purpose, mission and vision – that you can set some clear goals for the brand (these may be both short term and long term).

1. What are the top three things you are trying to achieve with the brand?

2. Where do you sit currently with these? What is your current state? What is the metric for measuring this and what's the benchmark you're starting from?

3. What is your future state and by when does this need to be in place or cemented? What are the metrics for measuring this?

4. What is the end result of these goals happening? How will you know when you have achieved them or are they an ongoing process?

It may be helpful to utilise the following framework (which incorporates gap analysis – the idea of looking at the gap that exists between current and desired states in business) to map this out.

Goal: To move from X (current state) to Y (future state) by (deadline) so that (outcome).

You want to ensure that the goals you set support the overall vision and mission of the company. They should also remain visible and be something you can easily refer to and be measured against.

Let's move on to one of my all-time favourite elements of a brand: values and beliefs.

Authenticity:
Values and beliefs

As you will know by now, I'm someone who massively believes in aligning your values and your brand, in standing for something and allowing that to influence the way you run your business and what it offers the world.

If you have never defined your brand values, or have values that may not be relevant for your brand anymore, you'll want to start with a basic brand values activity.

There are numerous ways to define your core brand values. I'll walk you through three of the most common and useful activities.

Values checklist

Most people know the values they want at the core of the brand they're building. This first activity will help you tap into that inner knowledge. Figure 5.1 (page 100) shows a table with a list of values: simple, usually single words that make you FEEL something. Surrounding them, or alongside, are other words that just don't hit the same spot.

For example, when I started my business, I knew 'freedom' was a huge part of what I was trying to achieve. This incorporated:

- freedom for myself (as selfish as that may seem, that was a huge component of why I quit a well-paid executive role and started a company)

- freedom for the people I was working with (i.e. them not feeling like they were giving up every minute in their day to test out marketing ideas)

- freedom for all (by helping brands with their marketing and content strategies I could also input my beliefs around diversity in the creative fields and have a say over the choice of models, photographers, videographers and stylists)

- freedom for my children and younger people around me (who might, through my company and the relationship I had to my work, see another possibility outside of working 24/7 to hit a financial goal).

This value of freedom spoke to me at the very beginning and it has been something at the forefront of what we offer, how we work and who we bring into the company, ever since.

Business *to* Brand

Figure 5.1 **Values checklist**

	✓		✓		✓
ACCOUNTABILITY		FAIRNESS		LOVE	
ACHIEVEMENT		FAITH		LOYALTY	
ADVENTURE		FAME		MEANINGFUL WORK	
AFFECTION		FAMILY		MONEY	
AFFECTIVE		FITNESS		NATURE	
AMBITION		FREEDOM		ORDER	
AUTHENTICITY		FRIENDSHIP		PASSION	
AUTHORITY		FUN		PEACE	
AUTONOMY		GENEROSITY		PERFECTION	
BEAUTY		GRATITUDE		PERSONAL DEVELOPMENT	
BEING THE BEST		GROWTH		PLEASURE	
CALMNESS		HAPPINESS		QUALITY	
CAREER		HARD WORK		RECOGNITION	
CHALLENGE		HEALTH		REPUTATION	
COMMUNICATIONS		HEART		RESPECT	
COMMUNITY		HELPING PEOPLE		SECURITY	
COMPASSION		HELPING SOCIETY		SERVICE	
COMPETENCY		HUMILITY		SPIRITUALITY	
CONNECTIONS		IMAGINATION		STABILITY	
CONSISTENCY		INDEPENDENCE		STATUS	
CONTRIBUTION		INNOVATION		SUCCESS	
COURAGE		INTEGRITY		TEACHING	
CREATIVITY		INTELLIGENCE		TEAMWORK	
CURIOSITY		INTIMACY		TRANSPARENCY	
DEPENDABILITY		INTUITION		TRAVEL	
DEPTH		JUSTICE		TRUST	
DETERMINATION		KINDNESS		VALUE	
ECONOMY		KNOWLEDGE		VISION	
EDUCATION		LEADERSHIP		WARMTH	
EMPATHY		LEARNING		WEALTH	
ENERGY		LEGACY		WISDOM	

Look through the list of values and consider the top ten values for the brand you are building. Then ask yourself why you have chosen these values.

Now, cull this list down to five to six values. It's important at this stage to consider why you are dropping certain values and why you are prioritising those that will stay.

Then, for each value, consider how your brand shows up authentically in alignment with it and how you might capture that in one succinct sentence.

For example:

Value: Freedom

The freedom of time, choice, inclusion and meaning.

Continue to do this for all of the values. If you're finding it hard to stick to just one sentence, that's okay. Many brands elaborate further on each value.

An example of this is Patagonia who, on the eve of its fiftieth anniversary in 2022, updated its core values to include quality, integrity, environmentalism, justice and not being bound by convention.

Here is how it elaborated on the first three. (For the full set of Patagonia's core values, check out patagonia.com/core-values)

- **Quality:** Build the best product, provide the best service and constantly improve everything we do. The best product is useful, versatile, long-lasting, repairable and recyclable. Our ideal is to make products that give back to the Earth as much as they take.

- **Integrity:** Examine our practices openly and honestly, learn from our mistakes and meet our commitments. We value integrity in both senses: that our actions match our words (we walk the talk), and that all of our work contributes to a functional whole (our sum is greater than our parts).

- **Environmentalism:** Protect our home planet. We're all part of nature, and every decision we make is in the context of the environmental crisis challenging humanity. We work to reduce our impact, share solutions and embrace regenerative practices. We partner with grassroots organisations and frontline communities to restore lands, air and waters to a state of health; to arrest our addiction to fossil fuels; and to address the deep connections between environmental destruction and social justice.

Writing your own values

When it comes to uncovering and defining your brand values, it may help to consider wedding vows. (If you're totally opposed to the concept of marriage, then consider any sort of commitment where you'll need to make a promise to someone.)

For some people (I'm raising my hand), using traditional vows works well. They are tried and tested and can take the pressure off of coming up with your own vows (that could date, or feel cringey years later). Others may want the opportunity to really create something original with their vows, something that defines who they are as individuals, and as a couple, and shows their creative flair. In the same way, your brand values may be something you want to define through a selection of terms from a values checklist or be values you wish to write and create in your own unique way.

Another way to define your brand values is to create them from scratch, much like you would your own wedding vows. You may decide to start with a word dump, creating a list of words and phrases that suit your brand and align with its purpose, vision and mission. This can be a fantastic exercise to do in a group, so if you're fortunate enough to have staff get them involved.

An example of values created in this way are those of Warby Parker. In a 2022 Impact Report Executive Summary, Warby Parker defined its eight core values as follows:

1. Inject fun and quirkiness into everything we do

   - Take our work and our impact seriously (but not ourselves)
   - Help others have fun

2. Treat others as they want to be treated

   - Design with empathy
   - Have a positive attitude

3. Pursue new and creative ideas

   - Embrace change and uncertainty
   - Continually challenge ourselves

4. Do good

   - Impact the world in a meaningful way
   - Value our customers, our peers, the community, and the environment
   - Practice gratitude

5. Take action
   - Set ambitious goals and measure results
   - Take the first step
6. Presume positive intent
   - Trust but verify
7. Lead with integrity
   - Be honest
   - Give and take direct feedback
8. Learn. Grow. Repeat.

Your brand is exactly that – *your brand* – and the way you phrase and come up with your values is entirely up to you. Be as creative, bold, personal or experimental as you like so long as your values hold meaning and are genuinely authentic.

Your belief statements

The last activity that can help when it comes to uncovering and defining your brand's values and beliefs is to focus on your belief statements.

What are the core beliefs that guide your brand? What are the beliefs that help people believe it to be authentic? How do these beliefs guide everything from the offers your brand creates through to the way people feel when they interact with your company?

One way to start mapping this out is to spend some time considering what it is that you and your staff believe when it comes to your brand and the elements that define it. Could you write down a list of the top twenty beliefs you hold when it comes to your brand – its vision, its mission, its audiences, its creations, its goals? Could others? Is it obvious?

Have a go.

Get out a blank piece of paper or open a Google/Word document and write out these statements, each starting with 'I believe' or 'We believe'.

You may wish to set yourself the task of writing ten to twenty of these statements or writing as many as you can within a certain time period (e.g. 15 minutes).

When you have finished, consider which ones really jump out as being in complete alignment with the brand you're building. If you have staff doing this, collate all of the answers and ask as a group: Which of these define us? Which of these work well with what we are trying to achieve?

Business *to* Brand

Here are some examples:

- Aesop: 'We believe unequivocally that well-considered design improves our lives.'

  This belief is evident in every area of the brand, from its impeccably designed global stores and product packaging, through to the design of its formulations and considered layout of its Australian head office in Collingwood, Victoria.

- Coco Flip: 'We believe in quality, not quantity. We believe a considered purchase is a purchase for life.'

  This belief underpins the Australian furniture and lighting design brand which for more than a decade has specialised in crafting unique, made-to-order pieces that journey through numerous master craftspeople before reaching customers' homes all over the world.

Outlining your brand beliefs is not just helpful for your own clarity over the direction your brand will take in a range of areas, it is also one of the key ways that audiences connect and favour one brand over another.

Earlier, I mentioned a sense of belonging as a key human psychological need. When we feel we share the same values and beliefs as a brand, we also tap into this psychological need to belong. This is how community is cultivated and, if done authentically and not in a manipulative way, can be one of the greatest assets a brand can attain.

Value alignment

Once you have your list of values, I want you to interrogate how well your brand is aligned with these values, both from an external perspective (i.e. what your customers/clients would think) and an internal perspective (i.e. what your staff, stakeholders, manufacturers, suppliers, contractors and subcontractors would think).

Using the table in Figure 5.2 on the opposite page (and the example in the first line), consider your own brand values and how well they are aligned externally and internally. Rate this out of ten for your current state, where 1 = misaligned and 10 = in total alignment.

Then consider examples of how these show up. Ideally – and it may take some time – you should be able to easily identify at least five examples of how the brand is externally and internally aligned with each of its core values.

Figure 5.2 **Value alignment for brand**

COMPANY ALIGNMENT	EXTERNAL ALIGNMENT SCORE AND EXAMPLE	INTERNAL ALIGNMENT SCORE AND EXAMPLE
Freedom	7/10: We actively celebrate causes which promote freedom in terms of access, equality, equity, opportunity and beliefs. We use inclusive language and collaborate/ partner with experts in this space.	4/10: Our latest annual reviews show a large percentage of people who marked 3/10 when asked how free they feel at work to contribute, speak out against things or work in more flexible ways.

Business *to* Brand

Once you have worked through the first alignment table, it's time to consider this from the viewpoint of you as the founder using the table in Figure 5.3 on the opposite page. For example, if I purport to align with the value of 'Freedom', what does that actually mean for my own freedom? How truly aligned am I – as the brand founder – with this value?

- Do I have enough time off?
- Do I feel I can turn away work because the financial buffers are in place or do I feel I have no choice and must take on everyone who contacts us?
- Do I feel free to miss work if my children are unwell?
- Do I feel free to support the causes I want within this business?
- Do I feel free to speak up to those I work with?
- Do I feel that I'm contributing in some way to the freedom of future generations to not be burdened by the challenges currently facing our planet?

Remember, it is about building an authentic brand, and the brand founder or leader is crucial in maintaining that trust and connection between brand and audience. All too often we see leaders of companies and brands come into the spotlight for saying one thing in their professional lives and doing quite the opposite when they think no one is looking.

Don't be that person.

This can be one of the most confronting things for business owners to realise, but in order to operate an authentic brand and sustain it well into the future, your business activity, actions and voice need to be in genuine alignment with your values. One of the quickest ways to disengage and lose trust with your audience is to showcase your brand values externally while having next to no alignment internally. This screams of inauthenticity and immediately lowers trust. For example, it is very common for companies to purport to be championing 'diversity' or 'equality' externally by using models of all shapes, ages, sizes and skin tones in campaigns to sell their clothes, and yet internally this diversity is not reflected in staff. Another example is the amount of companies that claim to have 'female equality' as a value and yet don't have a safe and secure place for returning mothers to pump their breastmilk apart from toilet cubicles. If you are seeking to create a brand that people can trust, grow with and stay loyal to, being internally aligned with the values you put out into the world is absolutely essential.

Figure 5.3 **Value alignment for founder**

INDIVIDUAL VALUE	INTERNAL ALIGNMENT SCORE AND EXAMPLE
Freedom	2/10: I have no time and am saying yes to every client regardless of whether they align with us or not

Once you have your values you will want to ensure that these are made clear to everyone who comes into contact with the brand. For staff, these values will need to be incorporated right from the very first interview or connection with potential candidates (or even earlier at the point of recruitment ads being written up), through to staff onboarding, weekly 1:1s, reviews and every other touchpoint. We will discuss this more in chapters 6 and 7, but for now consider how these values are brought to life every day within the brand, rather than simply being written somewhere and never looked at again.

For those who don't work within the brand, the values may well appear on your various touchpoints from in-store and point-of-sale signage, through to your website, welcome email sequences and media kits.

It may be helpful at this stage to revisit the buyer cycle (page 37) and consider how your values are externally and internally aligned at each stage.

After you have thought about your own brand values through the lens of the buyer cycle, work through these questions:

- Are the brand values clear for someone just becoming aware of the brand?

- Are the brand values obvious when researching the brand?

- Are the brand values a core part of your evaluation marketing and communications?

- Are the brand values showcased within the path to, and at the point of, purchase?

- Are the brand values in alignment in the post-purchase stage and do they help create advocates for your brand?

Business *to* Brand

If you're a creative thinker or someone who likes to learn through visuals, you might want to imagine your brand as the car, and the purpose, vision, mission and values as each of the four tyres that help it to move along.

Should I use my own personal values for my brand?

This is a question that comes up a lot, and for many small business owners their core brand values will have some crossover with their own individual personal values.

Here, what you want to do is interrogate each value against the overall vision and mission of the company.

For example, I may well have a personal value of affection, but that is not a core brand value for My Daily Business. That is, at this current moment in time, not something that is in alignment with the overall vision and mission for the brand.

If you're finding this difficult, look at your list of values and ask yourself if you would like your brand to be the go-to company for this particular value. In the case of My Daily Business and the value of affection, my answer would be 'no'.

By now you should have an idea of the core brand values that will attract and retain your audience, guide your business activity and strengthen the impact your brand has.

Once you are happy with your core brand values, read on.

Authenticity: Creations

When we talk about the word 'creations' in a brand sense, we are referring to the outputs of the brand, which could be its business model, revenue streams, and overall products and services on offer. The very title of this book is all about shifting from the idea of being simply a purely transactional business to becoming a brand. While there is nothing at all wrong with simply remaining a business – and most companies inevitably will – it is your brand that will set you apart not only emotionally and psychologically in the minds of your consumers, but also – for better or worse – financially.

I mentioned in Chapter 2 how much a brand comes down to perception – the perception that the brand is attempting to create, cultivate and, in some ways, control and that the recipient (i.e. your audience) believes. You can see this perception manifest in a plethora of ways, but one of the most obvious is the discrepancy in price between two objects which, objectively, are of the same value.

Let's take, for example, a leather couch (or sofa as some may call it). Or, to get even more specific, let's say it's a three-seater black couch in a mid-century modern style.

Brand A wants to create the perception of a value-for-money brand, the type of big-box place you might choose to buy from if furnishing your first rental after moving out of your childhood home, filling out an investment property or an Airbnb rental, or kitting out your office's foyer.

Brand B prides itself on being the well-made, well-priced brand. That is, it stands by its products. It may not be the cheapest, but it won't be the most expensive either. It doesn't tend to talk about its people or designers, but you know it'll be a quality product you end up with. When you buy from it you're making a smart decision. This is the sort of place you may well be happy to tag on social media. Quality goods at a decent price.

Brand C really promotes the story behind the couch. From the local designers who lovingly crafted its designs through to the myriad of craftspeople manufacturing it right through to the customer service and delivery team who install it. The entire journey is seamless and stress-free and the feeling is one of luxury. It comes with a cleaning cloth made from 100% recycled materials and a handwritten thank you card. From the moment you purchase it you feel excited – not only to have it in your home, but also to show it off to friends, to relay the story of the entire experience and to have something from this brand in your home. Yes, it takes a little longer to arrive, but it's Brand C, right? It's worth it.

Which of these brands – A, B or C – would you expect to be the least expensive? Which would be the most expensive?

The answers are quite obvious and yet we will often not even realise the subtle ways we are being influenced to buy or connect with one brand over another. After all, all three brands solve the problem of 'I need a couch' but only one solves the problem of 'I want to buy a locally designed couch that's also been ethically manufactured'.

Thinking about your own brand, consider the following questions:

- What problem does your brand solve through its products, services and experiences?
- How does this differ from others in the market?
- How is this showcased to your audience?
- And how do your vision, mission and values impact the way your products and services are offered and the price at which they are charged?

When it comes to creating genuine authenticity there has to be an alignment between the products and services you offer, your pricing strategy and your brand's purpose, vision, mission and values.

In my very early twenties I spent a summer learning about clothing manufacturing at a Melbourne-based factory that had been booming decades earlier, but whose customers had reduced with the increase of cheaper offshore alternatives. The perception was – and I would say still is – that if you wish to get clothing manufactured within a country like Australia you should expect to pay more than if it were to be done offshore, even if the offshore facility ticks every single box when it comes to labour costs, ethical audits and impeccable standards of production.

One thing to get clear on as early as you can is how your business makes money and how these revenue streams align with your brand. Think of this like the background work I was doing with the architects for my desired home extension. By creating a literal blueprint with the architects in the early stages, we were hoping to negate as many problems as possible down the line. Too often I see business owners who have not considered their revenue streams at all, or not done so early enough to ensure they align with the overall authenticity of their brand.

For example, let's say you're in the business of designing websites and your brand is all about slow living. You tend to attract business owners in aligned spaces (e.g. yoga, nutrition, meditation, doula services, mindfulness and breathwork).

Your mission may be: To help people slow down in a world that wants them to speed up.

Your values may include: freedom, relationship-building, connection, integrity and mindfulness.

It would not be in alignment with your brand for the business to be pumping out websites within one week, all created by someone remotely that you are paying $3 an hour to, while charging your clients thousands per project.

And yet these businesses exist.

What we are wanting to build here is a brand – and an authentic one at that.

In this instance, the brand vision, mission and values would be better suited to a business model where the client is first nurtured and connected with via a series of workshops before designs are created and presented in an open forum, free for dialogue and idea exchange to take place. The process, in alignment with 'slow living', may even go one step further and incorporate hand-drawn illustrations, the creation of a brand-new font that mirrors the founder's own handwriting and the use of tech platforms that are somehow giving back to the planet and people. When the website is launched there may be an in-person celebration, with locally grown food and wine, done in a way that represents deep human connection. The cost of all of this then needs to be factored into the services on offer.

This is where understanding your business model and how you actually make your money becomes super important. Financial stability is key for any business and is particularly important when building a brand so the business can survive long enough to have a real impact. Much like the work with my architect, this is one of the key steps to discuss, uncover, analyse and map out before getting further into the development of your brand.

So how do you do this?

Money-mapping

One quick way is a basic money-mapping exercise, in which you look at the various revenue streams in your business and ensure that:

- the revenue streams add up to your total Thrive Figure as a business

- the revenue streams align with your vision and mission

- the pricing structure of these aligns with your values and beliefs.

(This last point can be one that many people struggle with, particularly if their brand archetype errs more on the side of the Everyman or the Caregiver rather than the Creator or the Ruler.)

Let's discuss these now.

A whole book could be written about coming up with the Thrive Figure for your business (and it's something I cover in a bit more detail in my first book *Passion. Purpose. Profit.* and a lot more detail in our self-paced online Money Mapping course, available at mydailybusiness.com/courses).

For now, it's important to understand that for any business to have a chance of financial success, those leading it must be aware of two figures.

1. **Survive Figure:** This is the base level that the business – and you as its founder – needs purely to survive and pay wages, bills, commercial rent, subscriptions, base-level manufacturing and so forth.

2. **Thrive Figure:** This is your Survive Figure + all the things you would like to incorporate into the business to achieve your goals such as hiring more staff, investing in a larger space, paying better wages, adding to your pension/401K/superannuation, investing in causes that are meaningful to your business, employing consultants that can help you achieve greater impact, and further development of your website or physical premises.

Once you have your Thrive Figure you want to consider all of your revenue streams.

For a product-based business this may include your online store, physical store, wholesale, subscriptions, white labelling, design development, collaboration/limited edition lines and consulting.

For a service-based business, such as a graphic design studio, revenue streams may include website design, branding design, social media packages, retainer packages, done-for-you packages, do-it-yourself courses and templates.

For each stream, add in a financial goal – one that has been considered against things such as previous sales and knowledge of the revenue stream, number of clients and realistic time available.

For example, a business may have $80,000 against website design as its goal, knowing that the maximum number of projects it can take on in one calendar year is 10 and that on average most people spend $8000 for their website design (i.e. 10 x $8000 = $80,000).

Do this for all of your revenue streams and ensure they match, or at least come close to, your Thrive Figure as shown in Figure 5.4 on the opposite page.

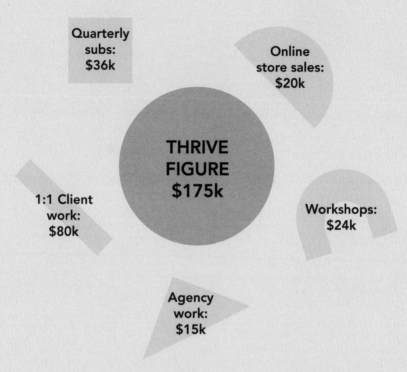

Figure 5.4 **Example money map for a graphic design brand**

Quarterly subs: $36k

Online store sales: $20k

THRIVE FIGURE $175k

1:1 Client work: $80k

Workshops: $24k

Agency work: $15k

You can see in the diagram that all of the revenue streams add up to the Thrive Figure in the middle. This is your goal.

The next key activity is to ensure that the revenue streams align with your vision and mission because we are building a brand here, not just a business.

Against each revenue stream, ask yourself (or together with your team):

- How does this revenue stream reflect our brand purpose?

- How does this revenue stream reflect our brand vision?

- How does this revenue stream reflect our brand mission?

- How does this revenue stream reflect our brand values and beliefs? (Example value: freedom; example revenue stream: online courses.)

Remember, brand is about authenticity. There should be no revenue stream that feels off-brand, no matter how financially appealing it may be.

Lastly, at this early stage, you want to consider the pricing strategy for your products, services and experiences. This can be a difficult thing to consider for

Business *to* Brand

many small business owners and it's something that may change slightly when we look at your audience later in this chapter, and at your positioning and competitor analysis in Chapter 6.

For now, consider all of the work you have done to this point. How does this impact your pricing strategy?

For example, let's say you're in the business of athletic apparel for people seeking to get back into nature. One of your key values is quality. Another is integrity.

Your apparel would need to be manufactured using quality materials and paying the garment workers a living wage so that you can operate with integrity. Given your brand is about getting people back into nature, you may also decide that you don't want to be using materials that are ravaging the earth, utilising huge volumes of water and/or that cannot easily be recycled. Furthermore, you may decide that you will offset carbon emissions from the freight flights that bring your items from the factory to other countries by donating or partnering with an environmental not-for-profit. All of these things – which, unfortunately, are not how most apparel businesses operate – need to be factored into the cost of each product and the end price you put on it.

The statement I hear most from clients when discussing pricing strategy is, 'But that would make things so expensive that no one would pay for it.' If this is how you genuinely feel, it's time to revisit why you're in business and what sort of impact you're hoping to have. Yes, you need to make a living and the business must be profitable to continue, but this does not always equate to doing things as cheaply as possible.

One brand that is transparent (at least at the time of writing this!) is Everlane, the US apparel brand that outlines the exact costs of its pieces on its website. It is easy to see the mark-up and, at times, it will run 'pay what you like' campaigns in which its audience can pay anything above the cost price of the piece. By doing this, it is showcasing the cost of the products, made in what it states are ethical supply chains, and also the cost that Everlane needs to charge on top of this to cover its own overheads and remain profitable.

Determining your prices can be one of the hardest parts of starting or scaling a business. By working through the questions below you may become clearer on your overall pricing strategy and how the work you have done until this point may impact where you wish to sit.

- When it comes to pricing, what are your greatest fears?
- What does this mean for your overall vision?
- How does your pricing strategy reflect your values and beliefs?

Understanding your revenue streams and how you make money (including the pricing strategy around each offer) is key to being able to create something sustainable. Even if this feels uncomfortable, it's crucial to work through this before continuing.

Brand architecture

Another element to consider when it comes to the creations of your brand and your business model is to think about the potential expansion or growth of the brand you are building. This concept is known as brand architecture.

Will you develop sub-brands in the years to come, or do you already have some now? Will you have other companies that sit alongside yours but are known by entirely different brand names? Will you need one parent brand name with room for other sub-brands?

When it comes to brand architecture there are four main categories:

1. **Monolithic:** This is where you have one master brand (e.g. Apple) and various product lines or sub-brands underneath it (e.g. Apple Podcasts, Apple TV, Apple Music, Apple iPhones).

2. **Pluralistic:** This is where you have one parent brand (e.g. LVMH) but the sub-brands or categories underneath it are independent brands (e.g. FENTY BEAUTY, Tiffany & Co., Hennessy, TAG Heuer). In many cases, you may not even realise the sub-brands are part of a parent company.

3. **Endorsed:** This is where you will have a parent brand (e.g. Marriott) that has sub-brands that are 'endorsed' by the parent brand (e.g. Courtyard by Marriott). Each of the sub-brands has its own identity but this is strengthened by its relationship with the parent brand.

4. **Hybrid:** This is where you have a parent brand that has perhaps acquired the sub-brands in some way, such as through mergers and acquisitions (e.g. Facebook acquiring Instagram then changing its parent brand name to Meta). It can be beneficial to keep the brand identity, mission, vision and values of acquired brands, so as to not confuse its audience, but also to strengthen the reputation and power (for want of a better word) of the parent brand.

For example, let's imagine that you have a website design agency called Woven Webs. You may decide to expand into the design of physical stores, and so you create another brand called Woven Stores. This may then lead you to create a parent brand (Woven) with sub-brands underneath (Woven Webs and Woven Stores).

When assessing your creations and building your foundations for an authentic brand, it helps to consider the ideal brand architecture most suited to the brand you're building.

Authenticity: Audience

This may be the last element under authenticity in the ACE brand model, but it is by no means the least important. In fact, defining your audience is one of the absolutely KEY things you will do when building a brand or transforming an existing business into one.

I have been helping companies and businesses define their audiences since 2001 when I started at an advertising agency in the East End of London and had to come up with an audience profile of one of the nearby council groups.

Since then I have been involved in conversations, workshops and strategy meetings on this same topic for more than two decades. I have witnessed myriad ways to uncover and define audiences and even more 'key questions' to ask. These include:

- Who is it we're aiming to connect with?
- Why would they choose us over an alternative?
- What do they most need?
- What helps them feel connected?
- What is their own 'why' and does it align with our mission, vision and values?
- What is a typical day in their life like?
- What's their biggest pleasure in life?
- What are their core values?
- What religion do they ascribe to or what spiritual beliefs do they hold?
- How old are they?
- How did they last vote?
- Are they single, in a couple, married, in a throuple?
- What are their core beliefs?
- What's their biggest fear?
- Do they care about politics?
- What would they eat for breakfast?

- What's their greatest regret?
- What's their most embarrassing desire?
- What would their last meal be?
- What's their #1 dance track?
- How would their friends describe them?
- What's their all-time favourite film?

And so on and so on …

Defining your audience can be an overwhelming task, but it doesn't need to be. Being authentic is about remembering that at EVERY single stage of interacting with your business, you have one human connecting with another. This starts by not only understanding the demographics of your audience (such as age, location, occupation and relationship status – although some of these, like age, are becoming redundant for some industries. Take fashion, for example. Social norms, which used to dictate things like how short a woman could wear a dress over a certain age, have changed so that fashion brands may well be targeting teenagers and women over seventy with the same fashion range) but also their psychographics (such as attitudes, aspirations, hopes, dreams, opinions and interests).

Let's look at Maslow's hierarchy of needs (see Figure 5.5 on page 119), a framework which was created by American psychologist Abraham Maslow in 1943. The hierarchy of needs is usually visually represented by a triangle wherein you have a hierarchy of human needs, with each one (from the base up) needing to be fulfilled before the one above can even begin to be attained. (In 2019, Todd Bridgman, Stephen Cummings and John Ballard published their work in the *Academy of Management Learning and Education*. They suggested that Maslow never actually created the visual triangle representation, rather that this visual was first used by a management consultant in the 1960s.)

Business *to* Brand

> '*Being authentic is about remembering that at EVERY single stage of interacting with your business, you have one human connecting with another.*'

Safety and security are key in the hierarchy of needs, second to our most basic physiological needs. Keep this in mind when we consider Qantas, an Australian airline known for its approach to travel, design and cuisine. It is also well regarded as one of the statistically safest airlines in the world (a fact made famous by Dustin Hoffman's character Raymond Babbitt in the 1988 film *Rain Man*). Many people would initially connect with the Qantas brand via their need for safety and the perception that Qantas is a safe airline to choose.

Consider where your audience sits in the hierarchy. Then consider what you are offering in relation to your brand. Is it love and belonging? Is it self-esteem? Is it purely safety and security? Which section of Maslow's hierarchy does what you offer most apply to?

Figure 5.5 **Maslow's hierarchy of needs**

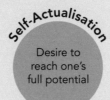

Self-Actualisation

Desire to reach one's full potential

Esteem

Respect,
Freedom,
Self-esteem,
Status,
Recognition

Love & Belonging

Intimacy, Family,
Friendship, Connection

Safety & Security

Personal security,
Employment, Resources

Physiological Needs

Food, Water, Shelter, Sleep, Clothing, Air

Business *to* Brand

You can develop this further by mapping out your ideal audience in a buyer persona or audience profile.

Your buyer persona can incorporate a million different questions. A simple one I have created that has helped countless small business clients and larger corporates alike includes the following areas shown below in Figure 5.6.

Figure 5.6 **Example buyer persona**

Name/Nickname (Audience Segment)

AGE:	**POLITICAL LEANING:**
FEELS-LIKE AGE:	**STRESS LEVEL:** /10
RELATIONSHIP:	**DREAM JOB:**
OCCUPATION:	**#1 DANCE TRACK:**
INCOME:	**BIGGEST REGRET:**
RELIGION:	**BIGGEST FEAR:**

BELIEFS:	**DESIRES:**
PAINS:	**FEARS:**
PLEASURES:	

DESCRIPTIVE ACCOUNT OF A DAY IN THE LIFE:

WHAT FRUSTRATES THEM ABOUT YOUR INDUSTRY?

3 QUESTIONS THEY'D NEED THE ANSWER TO FIRST BEFORE ENGAGING:

WHAT IS THEIR WHY AND HOW DOES IT RELATE TO YOUR BRAND'S WHY?

OTHER BRANDS THEY LOVE AND WHY:

OTHER BRANDS THEY DISLIKE AND WHY:

You'll notice a question in the figure that often stumps people.

What is your audience's why? What inspires them? How does this align with your brand's why?

Business *to* Brand

To get to the heart of some of these questions you may wish to utilise a framework known as the empathy map (Figure 5.7 below).

Created by Dave Gray (the founder of School of the Possible and author of *Gamestorming*), not the singer by the same name who penned some of the best songs of 1998 #HelloWhiteLadder), this framework is used to understand the feelings, thoughts, actions and expressions of a certain group of people. For example, for a start-up introducing a new area of an app, these may be existing users; while for a large retail group introducing a new brand, these may be people its other brands have not yet interacted with.

Figure 5.7 **The empathy map**

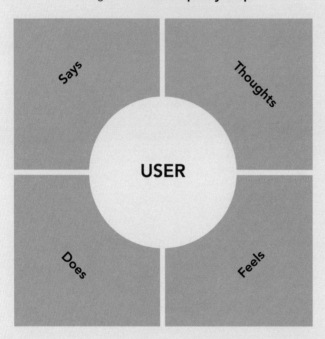

In 2017 Gray created the empathy map canvas (Figure 5.8 on the opposite page), which goes a bit further in helping people really understand, and have empathy for, a chosen group.

By now you will understand just how important genuine, authentic connection is between your brand and everyone who encounters it, and one of the best ways to cultivate connection is through empathy.

Consider your ideal audience, or one of your key audience segments (you may well have a few), for your brand. Then, using the prompts in Gray's empathy map canvas, work through all of the questions until you feel you have a solid understanding of your ideal audience. You can download your own version of the empathy map canvas to work through via gamestorming.com/empathy-mapping/.

Start with authenticity

Figure 5.8 **The empathy map canvas**

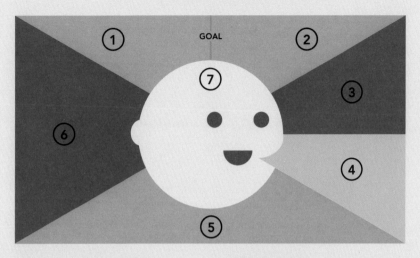

1. **WHO** ARE WE EMPATHISING WITH?
   Who is the person we want to understand?
   What is the situation they are in?
   What is their role in the situation?

2. WHAT DO THEY NEED TO **DO**?
   What do they need to do differently?
   What job(s) do they want or need to get done?
   What decision(s) do they need to make?
   How will we know they were successful?

3. WHAT DO THEY **SEE**?
   What do they see in the marketplace?
   What do they see in their immediate environment?
   What do they see others saying and doing?
   What are they watching and reading?

4. WHAT DO THEY **SAY**?
   What have we heard them say?
   What can we imagine them saying?

5. WHAT DO THEY **DO**?
   What do they do today?
   What behaviour have we observed?
   What can we imagine them doing?

6. WHAT DO THEY **HEAR**?
   What are they hearing others say?
   What are they hearing from friends?
   What are they hearing from colleagues?
   What are they hearing second-hand?

7. WHAT DO THEY **THINK** AND **FEEL**?
   Pains: What are their fears, frustrations
   and anxieties?
   Gains: What are their wants, needs, hopes
   and dreams?
   What other thoughts and feelings might motivate
   their behaviour?

Another area of audience mapping that doesn't always get attention at this stage of brand creation and one that can really help when it comes to choice of brand expression, marketing channels and connection points later on, is to consider where your ideal audience is placed in the wider social landscape.

Are they the first to jump in and give something new a try or do they possess more of a wait-and-see approach? Are they interested in products and services that have already hit the mainstream or do they avoid those entirely? Are they early in adopting brands in certain sectors (e.g. hospitality) and laggards when it comes to others (e.g. tech)?

You may well have a few audience segments and your answers may differ for these different groups. One framework that can help you consider where your audience is placed now and in the future in relation to your brand is the Rogers diffusion of innovations theory, which is often expressed via the Rogers diffusion curve (see Figure 5.9 on page 124).

Business *to* Brand

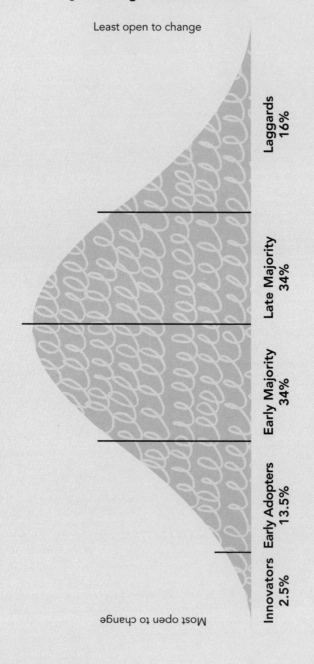

Figure 5.9 **Rogers diffusion curve**

Least open to change

Each group influences the one after them

Most open to change

Innovators 2.5%

Early Adopters 13.5%

Early Majority 34%

Late Majority 34%

Laggards 16%

Start with authenticity

Developed in 1962 by Everett M Rogers, the Rogers diffusion curve explains how new ideas, products, technologies or innovations spread and are adopted by individuals or groups within a society over time. It consists of five key groups, with each group being influenced by, and essentially following, the one before it.

1. **Innovators:** This is the group where a product, innovation or cutting-edge technology or brand will seep into first. Innovators are often risk-takers, willing to try new things just for the sake of being first and may have more disposable income than the average person (i.e. the cost of innovative products is usually greatest at the start – think Tesla and the iPhone when they first came out). Innovators are a small part of society, making up approximately 2.5% of the population.

2. **Early adopters:** This group is often considered to be 'the cool kids' in adopting a new style, trend, innovation, creation, brand or product. They are the ones you'll see wearing something before it hits the mainstream and are usually well connected, gaining insights from their friends and contacts who may well be in the innovator group. Early adopters make up 13.5% of the population.

3. **Early majority:** Not quite as daring as the early adopters, the early majority are happy to wait a little longer for proof of concept before they jump in. They need the innovators and early adopters to have demonstrated to them that whatever they're buying into, whether a trend or a product, is worth their time and somehow improves their life. This group is more cautious in making decisions around what they will and won't adopt. As the name suggests, the early majority make up a larger proportion of society, at around 34%.

4. **Late majority:** This group is a little more sceptical about newer innovations and trends and will really only jump in and adopt them once they have become widely adopted (aka mainstream). One of the main reasons people in this group will concede and adopt something new is usually down to social pressure or out of necessity (e.g. they need to join XYZ in order to use their favourite apps). Like the early majority, this group makes up around 34% of the population.

5. **Laggards:** We all know someone who will just not adopt an innovation until they are absolutely forced into doing so. This last group is often resistant to change and will only join in when there's no other choice. As a group they are generally the least open to change and the least likely to embrace new ideas. Laggards make up around 16% of the population.

Which group does your audience fit in with? How does this influence your brand?

Finally, when looking at your audience, ask yourself what their biggest reason is to believe in your brand?

Perhaps it's the extensive experience you have had in your field before starting the company, perhaps it's the unrivalled longevity your brand has established or perhaps it's because of the science behind your claims. Whatever the reason, you want to be clear on the most important elements that will help someone to believe in and trust your authentic brand.

This may be confirmed in more detail when you get to the positioning of your brand and how you express your brand through various communication touchpoints.

By now you should have a solid understanding of the elements that make up the authentic foundations of your brand, or the A in your ACE brand.

Together, these will act as the base upon which everything else can be created. As your brand grows and adapts or even changes in the years to come, you will want to revisit these elements that genuinely keep your brand authentic and ensure that they are tested, challenged and constantly reassessed to be in alignment with everything you do.

Authenticity is not something you can magically conjure up, or which results after a few exercises in a book. It is something that you work actively at upholding day in, day out. It is something that can build trust, strengthen connections and help bring your brand purpose to life. Commit to it. Challenge yourself and those who work within and around your brand to measure up to it constantly, and don't be afraid to change course when you feel yourself drifting away from its tracks.

TASKS TO CONSIDER

This was a MAMMOTH chapter with a lot to consider. Authenticity is a word so overused, particularly in the entrepreneurial space, that you may have started this chapter feeling like the term had been diluted and rendered obsolete. It's my hope that at this stage, especially if you have taken the time to really consider and work through the tasks and activities in the chapter, you are feeling more hopeful and grounded about authenticity when it comes to your brand.

Work through the following tasks or download them in a worksheet form online via the QR code below.

1. *Using the knowledge you have gained so far, work through the tasks for each of the authenticity elements:*

    - *Purpose*
    - *Vision*
    - *Mission*
    - *Values and beliefs*
    - *Creations*
    - *Audience.*

2. *Revisit your answers in Figure 3.5 (page 62) and look at how you originally ranked these six elements for your brand.*

3. *Now that you have done the work (or come back to this when you have), where would you rank yourself now?*

4. *How has this ranking changed? What further changes are necessary?*

5. *When will you take action on these? Get out the calendar and schedule this in.*

You may decide to jump right into Chapter 6 and the next stage in the ACE brand framework, or spend some more time to consider and work on all that you have learned from this chapter.

 Scan for digital worksheet

Business *to* Brand

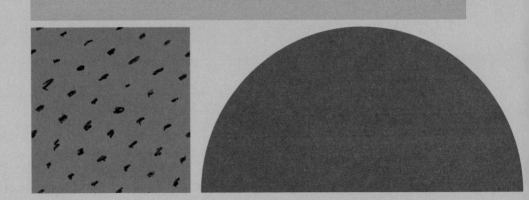

06.

Build with creativity

There are many things in life that make me happy, but among the top are organisation (even the perception of it) and colour in all of its glorious joyful abundance. I am someone who loves a good Google Sheet, colour-coded and clear in what it's trying to tell me. I am never without highlighters in the full spectrum of the rainbow and am known to make the owner of my local nail salon laugh at my constant attempt to have as many different colours used at any one time (#HelloRainbowNails).

Almost a decade ago and on the cusp of starting my own business, I was invited to a dinner with three amazing and ambitious women. During the conversation, one of the women opened up her handbag to get a tissue and I couldn't help but notice the quality of craftsmanship of her bag and also the attention to detail. Hidden inside the bag were numerous pockets, embossed with labels, for what was ideally to be placed inside: phone, passport, keys.

At the time I was working in an executive marketing role for one of the largest handbag and accessory brands in Australia with more than 100 stores across three countries. Prior to that I had worked for years as a fashion journalist and as the editor of two fashion magazines. In short, I had been looking at bags and images of different creations for many years, and yet something about this particular bag really stood out. When I asked my friend about the bag she relayed stories of the brand and what it stood for, the ethical way in which the pieces were manufactured and the quirky considerations that made them feel incredibly unique.

It's funny how you come across things you didn't know and then seem to see them everywhere, like a word you have never heard of and then see in the next article you read or overhear someone use while on your commute. The name of this brand – Anya Hindmarch – suddenly became one I would hear more and more about. At work, references to it came up in creative discussions. In my reading, examples of its campaigns would show up in respected publications. What had been until then the unknown became something very familiar. Over the next decade I watched as the Anya Hindmarch brand seemed to put out an endless array of winning collections, implement creative and curious campaigns, and work to change the way luxury items are created.

In Anya Hindmarch's book, *If In Doubt, Wash Your Hair* (a book I have recommended probably more than any other in recent times), the founder suggests that in place of 'brand', companies should consider the term 'behaviour' – to really question their own behaviour and how well it aligns with their vision and values, and how their behaviour reflects the company. If I needed another reason to fall in love with the brand, this was it. I couldn't agree more with her sentiments.

In 2023 I found myself back in London, ten years since I had last called that historic city home. Despite having limited time to visit with friends, see the sights and indulge in research for this book, I made sure that visiting the Anya Village was of top priority.

Build with creativity

'We can't ignore that so often our initial pique in curiosity with a brand is down to how its products and services visually appeal.'

Located in Pont Street, London, Anya Village includes a range of boutiques all representing the Anya brand. These include an ever-changing concept store, a flagship Anya Life store selling homewares and lifestyle pieces, The Collection Shop selling a curated edit of its main collection pieces, The Labelled shop which is like Disneyland for anyone into organisation and colour coding (#BothHandsUp), The Bespoke shop which was the first original Anya Hindmarch store to open in 1996 and offers bespoke customisable pieces, and the Anya Cafe, a delightful little corner cafe selling delectable pastries, cakes and sandwiches created in the likeness of the brand's well-known characters (think fish-shaped sandwiches and pastries shaped as hearts). Everything within the village has been considered so that it creates an incredibly consistent brand message – from the eyes on the tiny packets of sugar that come with your tea in the cafe, through to the level of craftsmanship within the Bespoke shop that makes you feel like you have stepped back in time, and the colourful exuberance and attention to detail in the Labelled shop. It's a celebration and embodiment of the brand and all it stands for.

As I visited each of the stores and dined in the Anya Cafe it all just worked together and genuinely embodied the Anya Hindmarch brand – considered, organised, colourful, unique and most of all, creative.

While my love affair with the Anya Hindmarch brand (and the woman herself) has deepened over the years due to the way the business is relentlessly working to change the way designer pieces are manufactured and repurposed, it can't go unnoticed that what initially attracted me to the brand was its aesthetic and organisational appeal.

This is where creativity, or the C in our ACE brand model, comes into play; the art of bringing your brand's vision, mission, purpose, creations and values to life in a way that not only attracts, but also engages and retains your ideal audience/s. We can't ignore that so often our initial pique in curiosity with a brand is down to how its products and services visually appeal.

Creativity is key for any brand to succeed. Problem-solving, cultivating a culture people actively want to be part of, advocating for change, championing innovation and finding ways to genuinely connect with your audiences – past, present and potential – all takes creativity. This is why the next stage of creating a meaningful ACE brand is to focus on the creative elements, the reasons why

Business *to* Brand

you'll stand out and how your position, personality and visual language can aid in genuine connection between your brand and its audience.

In the ACE brand model, creativity incorporates your brand's:

- positioning
- competition
- name and story
- personality and voice
- visual identity
- content.

While there are many additional elements that could sit under the umbrella of creativity when it comes to brand, these six elements are key to ensuring that you understand how to best attract, engage, retain and form genuine relationships with your ideal audience/s.

It's important to read and work through this entire chapter before hiring anyone, such as a graphic designer or design agency, to help. This will ensure you are clear on what you need and understand all the facets of creativity in brand, before bringing other people's opinions into the mix.

Ready to begin?

Creativity: Positioning

I'm a huge – and proud – fan of reality TV (go on, cast your judgements). I'm also a fan of thought-provoking documentaries, impeccable dramas and ultra-niche true crime investigations. But for this next element in building our authentic brand, it's important for you to know that I *know* reality TV.

Why?

Because in every single reality TV show there will be a cast that has been divided into 'characters'. You know, the villain/mean girl, the innocent/sweet one, the boss/fierce one, the aloof/ditzy one, the funny/easygoing one, the rebellious/fight-against-the-system one, the sexy/seductive one and the save the world/wise one (among others). Each of them has a position to play in the minds of the audience and in the narrative of the show.

In the same way, when people are deciding which brands to buy into and which brands define their own style, taste, values, interests and beliefs, they will be looking for markers that tell them how that brand is positioned in the market.

Now, the idea of positioning – how you want your business to be perceived by your chosen audience – has been around for decades (some believe as early as the 1920s), but it was really only brought to life and coined in relation to brands around the 1960s and 1970s through the work of former advertising executives, Al Ries and Jack Trout. The duo wrote about the concept in numerous industry publications in the late 1960s and early 1970s before publishing their first book on the topic, *Positioning: The Battle for Your Mind*.

According to Ries, positioning is a vehicle our mind uses to determine where something belongs and organise it into place. It is about how your audience distinguishes your brand from others in the market and the attributes they look for in order to be able to do this.

(If you really want to dive into this in more detail check out their book as well as the work of David Ogilvy, who some people say first came up with the concept a decade before Trout and Ries #OohControversy.)

It is important to consider how you want your brand to be perceived in the minds of your audience/s before getting stuck into your visual identity, brand voice or any sort of marketing strategy.

As Ries and Trout attest to, most of us think about the category of the product or service we want first (e.g. wedding photography, car, business coaching) before we think about the brand. What you want is for your brand to be the first thought of, or one of the first, in a particular category. For example, 'I need a wedding photographer (category) and I heard about this amazing woman on the *Modern Weddings* podcast who does this in our city. I really connected with her and feel she will do a great job because of X, Y and Z.'

It's the X, Y and Z in that thought process which is where positioning comes in.

One way to start working on this for your brand is to consider the important factors that come into play for your particular audience. For example, is cost one of the deciding factors? Experience? Exclusivity? Do they mind if your brand has locations all over the world or do they want to attach themselves to local brands specific to one particular part of the globe? Do they want to know you're aligned with a certain status or cool crowd to buy into your services or products? Or do they prefer you not to have those alignments? Do they want your brand because of its associations to a particular cause? Or do they want a brand that veers away from certain issues?

Brand positioning map

A method to begin working out these factors is to use what's called a brand positioning map. This is a visual representation, or map, of how your brand is positioned in relation to the key attributes your audience desires.

So, how does it work?

Start with a two-dimensional graph.

On the Y-axis (vertical) have one set of opposing attributes (or features) such as exclusive/mainstream, high cost/low cost or multi-location/single location. On the X-axis (horizontal) do the same with another set of opposing attributes such as high quality/low quality, utilitarian/luxurious or classic/modern. Once you have decided on your attributes for the X-axis and Y-axis, consider where your brand fits and map this in.

Depending on where your brand sits in its establishment, you may choose to plot where you are now and where you wish to be in the future. Or you may decide to map in where you believe your brand sits and, in another colour, where your audience perceives your brand to sit. Sometimes, as hard as it can be to confront (#GoodbyeEgo), there may be quite a chunky gap between the two markings.

Let's say, for example, your business sells stationery – not just any old stationery but ethically created stationery for people who love the old-school appeal of pen and paper but hate the idea of adding to landfill. You sell your stationery at a lower cost than others on the market as you want more people to choose to buy from ethically manufactured brands like yours. You may decide to have the following variables:

Y-axis: high cost/low cost

X-axis: mass produced/ethically produced

Consider where you are now, or your current positioning (red dot). If you feel it differs, also mark out how your brand is perceived by your audience currently based on audience feedback, or your audience positioning (yellow dot). Then map out where you want to be positioned in the minds of your audience/s in the near future, or your ideal positioning (blue dot). You may end up with something like the positioning in Figure 6.1 on the opposite page.

Figure 6.1: **Stationery positioning map**

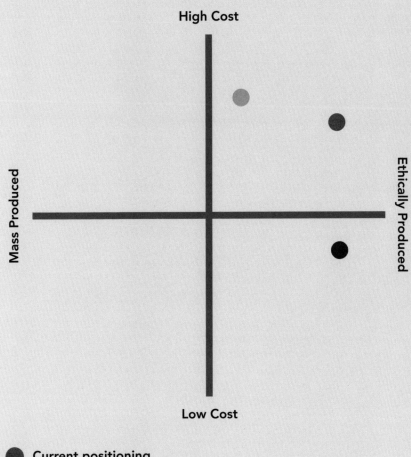

High Cost

Mass Produced

Ethically Produced

Low Cost

● Current positioning

● Ideal positioning

● Audience positioning

Business *to* Brand

The example on the previous page shows that in the minds of your audience, you're still too expensive for them to justify spending the money on vs buying cheaper, mass-produced stationery products from discount department stores. They also don't seem to know you're ethically produced so there is a mismatch between the messages you are putting out and what they are receiving.

Consider your own brand and the key attributes and features that are important to your audience and their perception of what it is you're offering. Then map out your X-axis and Y-axis, and mark out where you feel your brand sits. Repeat the entire process with other sets of attributes until you begin to really see where your brand fits in the market and in the minds of your audience.

At this stage, you may well be thinking, 'I don't know what my audience thinks'. If this is the case, you may want to validate your assumptions. This can be done in a variety of ways, including but not limited to:

- sending a survey using a tool like Google Forms or Typeform

- observing your audience in your physical locations or in another setting where they are interacting with your products/services

- creating a focus group of past clients/customers and engaging them prior to mapping out new collections, offers, experiences or product lines

- running polls using your social channels

- conducting feedback sessions.

In all cases, you not only want to be analysing the data and what it's telling you but also the detail in the data – the words and phrases people use when discussing your brand, the frustrations they may have with your industry and anything else that comes up. Map this information against what you have created in your brand positioning maps and see where and why it matches or differs.

Brand archetypes

The second task that can help with positioning is one we have already discussed briefly in Chapter 2, brand archetypes. You can revisit the visual representation of this in Figure 2.2 (page 34).

Given your work on Audience in Chapter 5, you should now have a clear understanding of who your audience/s is and what they desire from your brand (or one like it in the marketplace).

When considering your brand position, consider how you wish to be perceived and how looking at this through the lens of archetypes can help. This is not only from your perspective within the brand, but also (and sometimes more so) from the perspective of your audience/s. Which archetypes will most appeal to them and help them to form genuine connections with your brand?

Next, we discuss the twelve archetypes (divided into four main groups) and what each represents.

Seeking paradise

The three brand archetypes within this group are:

- **The Innocent:** This archetype is reminiscent of children – optimistic, hopeful, naive to some degree and wonderfully simple. This archetype is all about finding joy, harmony, doing the right thing and bringing positivity to situations. *Examples: Dove, Vicks*

- **The Sage:** This archetype is all about knowledge and wisdom and sharing that with others. Sage brands are often those that share education and help people understand how to do something better. They are also usually grounded in fact and uncovering the truth behind things and, as such, are thought of as experts. *Examples: Google, TED, Oprah*

- **The Explorer:** This archetype represents freedom and curiosity and is excited by adventure and uncovering new things. These brands are all about answering life's big questions: Why do we exist? What does a truly fulfilling life look like? This archetype is all about freedom, independence and exploration. *Examples: Patagonia, NASA, Jeep*

Leaving a legacy

The three brand archetypes within this group are:

- **The Outlaw:** This archetype is all about pushing boundaries, or breaking them altogether. It's about questioning convention and doing things your way. It's bold, courageous and powerful. Brands with this archetype often connect with community, inspiring others to live their own outlaw existence. *Examples: VICE, Harley Davidson*

- **The Magician:** This archetype is all about creating magic and transformation where others can't. This archetype is excited to merge intelligence and universal laws with mystery to create something innovative. Brands in this space tend to be charismatic, value innovation and celebrate curiosity at every corner. *Examples: Disney, Dyson, Sony*

- **The Hero:** This archetype represents the visionary that will work to make the world a better place. Like the lead role in a blockbuster action film, the hero will find a way to save things and will do so with risk, mastery and ambition. These brands come across as honest, brave and courageous. *Examples: Nike, Land Rover, Adidas*

Business *to* Brand

Building connection

The three brand archetypes within this group are:

- **The Lover:** This archetype is all about building intimacy and has a strong lean towards beauty, sensuality and passion. Brands in this space are often helping their audience connect and tap into their deepest desires and longings. It's all about building intimacy, closeness and desirable emotions. *Examples: Victoria's Secret, Louboutin, Dior*

- **The Jester:** This archetype is all about having fun with a lighthearted, upbeat, humorous approach to life. Brands in this space are usually entertainers of some sort and lift people up through wit, charm and positivity. It's all about living in the moment, celebrating sharp intellect through humour (even in response to serious situations) and interpreting events in surprising ways (think Oreo and its infamous Superbowl blackout tweet of 2013). *Examples: M&Ms, Oreo, Skittles*

- **The Everyman:** As the name suggests, this archetype is all about bringing simplicity and practicality to its audience. You know what to expect with Everyman brands and it's this consistency in what's delivered that elicits trust. They don't need to be the biggest or the boldest, but are relatable and reliable. While they can still innovate, it's delivered in a simple way that everyone can understand. *Examples: IKEA, Target, McDonald's*

Providing structure

The three brand archetypes within this group are:

- **The Caregiver:** This archetype is all about giving back, giving support and being seen as someone who helps. It's about having a community-minded approach to everything and looking at how we can do more for people and the planet. Caregiver brands are usually those with an altruistic outlook with a warm, approachable and friendly personality. *Examples: Who Gives a Crap, Design Can, UNICEF*

- **The Ruler:** This archetype is about control over chaos. It's about structure and usually this helps impact its power and dominance. Brands in this archetype are really looking to be the absolute best in class; they are confident, believe themselves to be experts and dedicated to their craft. Brands in this archetype usually offer security, safety and status. *Examples: Rolls-Royce, Rolex, Hugo Boss*

- **The Creator:** This archetype is all about bringing new things into the world and enjoying the process of creating as much as the outcome at the end of it. Creator brands are those that push the envelope, don't conform to what's expected and are trying to show what's possible if we dare to think outside of the box. *Examples: Apple, YouTube, LEGO*

Once you have identified the one to two archetypes that are most suited to your brand, consider your brand actions and offers to date.

- How closely do they align to these archetypes?

- What might need to change for these to be fully realised and for your audience to genuinely connect?

- Do they feel authentic? Do they feel both internally and externally aligned?

Once you have worked through the two positioning tasks, reflect on what else your audience may need to know before you become lodged into position in their minds.

- What is it about you that stands out? If you think about it in terms of dating, what would be the traits they find most appealing about your brand?

- How close/far are you from where you would like to be when it comes to your brand's positioning and the space it occupies in the minds of your audience?

When you're clear on all of the above, it's time to get stuck into the next step: reviewing the competition.

Creativity: Competition

Brand strategists often treat positioning and competitor analysis as one and the same thing. I tend to think of them as similar, yet different.

Here's a simple way of thinking about it. Your positioning, as you have just read, is all about the position you want to have in the minds of your audience. That is where you are positioned and why Poonum or Jonno might think of your brand first when it comes to making their decision. Competitor analysis is about taking this concept of positioning and analysing the key attributes that make you stand out in this way. It may be your:

- cost

- sense of community (e.g. causes you are aligned with)

- location

- size

- customer service

- experience

- price.

For example, let's say you're an online educator and you want to start selling courses. You may have heard of some brands and platforms that can help you with this (e.g. Kajabi, Teachable, Thinkific, LearnWorlds). Perhaps you have listened to some people on business podcasts who have used Kajabi, and so that brand is positioned in your mind as one of the best because, at least from what you have heard, it is popular with your business peers.

Your competitor analysis would then *compare* Kajabi with its competitors in the marketplace utilising features and metrics that are important to you. What would be the metrics you most want to compare across competing brands? Likewise, if your brand was in competition with, say, Kajabi, which metrics would most of your ideal audience use to compare them?

Now you can begin to conduct an analysis of where your brand sits and how well it is doing (via a series of metrics) compared to other brands in the market.

Competitive matrix

One of the first tasks you can do for competitor analysis is to complete a competitive matrix. For example, let's say you're a new high-end bakery brand that wants to steal market share, become known as the go-to brand for luxurious delicacies and be the best in the market in a particular location.

You may decide that most people in this imaginary location are seeking:

- service
- choice of goods (including gluten-free and dairy-free options)
- atmosphere
- fit-out/aesthetics
- seating
- coffee/tea options
- parking.

Let's also say that in this imaginary location, there are three other bakeries, two of whom are brands with communities that know them and one which isn't as well known and would be considered more as a business only, not a brand. What you will do now is compare the other three bakery brands to your own using the metrics you have deemed important to your audience (i.e. service, atmosphere, etc.).

To do this you first need to assign a weight to each metric and ensure, when all added up, the total for all weights = 1 or 100%. For example, if you have four metrics, each may be equally weighted 0.25 (or 25%), or they could be variants that together add up to 1 or 100% depending on the value assigned to the metric. For example, is the service in a bakery more important than the coffee/tea options? Is parking more important than the atmosphere? It can be hard to make a blanket judgement as parking may well be more important for a suburban bakery than a city-based bakery where public transport/cycling may be a more common mode of transportation.

For each brand/competitor score each metric out of a scale of 1–5, where 1 is the lowest possible score and 5 is the best possible score, and multiply this by the weight assigned to that metric. For example, if Brand A scored 4/5 for service and the weight of that metric is 0.2, it would have a total mark of 4 x 0.2 = 0.8.

Your competitive matrix may look like the one in Figure 6.2.

Figure 6.2 **Competitive matrix**

COMPETITOR	WEIGHT	BAKERY A	SCORE	BAKERY B	SCORE	BAKERY C	SCORE	YOUR BRAND	SCORE
SERVICE	0.2	4	0.8	3	0.6	2	0.4	4	0.8
CHOICE	0.1	3	0.3	2.5	0.25	2	0.2	5	0.5
ATMOSPHERE	0.1	1	0.1	1	0.1	1	0.1	3	0.3
FIT-OUT	0.1	2	0.2	1	0.1	1	0.1	3	0.3
SEATING	0.2	5	1	2	0.4	4	0.8	3	0.6
COFFEE/TEA	0.2	4	0.8	3	0.6	5	1	4	0.8
PARKING	0.1	5	0.5	1	0.1	1	0.1	1	0.1
TOTALS	1		3.7		2.15		2.7		3.4

Business *to* Brand

From this table you can easily see that while your brand isn't at the top in every factor – just yet – it surpasses the competition when it comes to the choices available, as well as fit-out and overall atmosphere. It may be these traits that you lead with when it comes to your messaging and marketing activities. The table also shows you who you need to be looking at when it comes to the competition (in this case, Bakery A).

You can also repeat this task but in place of factors such as service and parking, you can analyse your competitor's marketing activity, for example auditing their:

- website
- social media channels
- content mix (e.g. all text or a mix of video, audio, text)
- PR and media
- podcasts
- emails
- apps
- SMS activity
- physical marketing (e.g. in-store, billboards)
- influencers/ambassadors
- collaborations and partnerships.

You may also decide to look at their content themes – what are they aiming to be the go-to brand for? Which content themes are they trying to 'own' in the market?

SWOT analysis

Back in Chapter 3 we looked at a SWOT analysis for your own brand (page 56). You can repeat this SWOT analysis when looking at your competitors. Where do you differ? Where are you aligned? Where are their gaps? Where are their threats? If you want to revisit the key questions, refer back to page 57.

Competitor positioning map

Likewise, at the start of this chapter we looked at the positioning map for your brand and where you sit in the market based on differing attributes. You may wish to build on your brand positioning map by inputting five to ten of your competitors onto the map and charting where they sit in comparison to your brand. To revisit how to do this, check out Figure 6.1 (page 135).

Before moving on, it's important to reflect here on any biases you may have towards your own brand. We can often fail to see our own shortcomings, especially if we are new to the market or feel the product/service we offer is innovative and original ('Of course it's a 5/5, we're brilliant!'). Many small business owners don't necessarily have huge budgets to employ paid focus groups or work with a brand agency to set this up. If this is the case for you, consider the data you have access to that solidifies your answers. You may also consider asking clients/customers for input in return for a discount off their next purchase or a free gift.

Lastly, remember these are not 'set and forget' tasks. Your competitors are always changing and adapting, and so too are the needs of your audience. Therefore it is important to revisit your analysis every quarter or half-year to ensure you're not missing anything. Also, be sure not to rush this. You may well complete these tasks, give it a few days or a week then revisit them and check that they still feel accurate.

By now you should have a good understanding of how your brand, not just your business, is positioned and the elements that make it stand out from your competitors. With this in mind, the next step should be a little easier.

Creativity: Name and story

You may well be thinking, isn't it a little late in the piece to be deciding on my brand name and story? Well, depending on where you are in your business journey you may already have a name/story you love, or be looking for some help with a new brand name/story, or even to rebrand. Either way it's much easier to come up with a brand name/story, or change it in a rebrand, when you have done the initial work uncovering everything in Chapter 5 (from your vision and values, through to your authenticity markers and audience) as well as your positioning and competitive analysis.

Too often I see small business owners pay little attention to all of the above then end up with a brand name/story that doesn't actually align with their overall vision or the position they wish to occupy in the minds of their ideal (considered!) audience.

Brand name

So, what's in a name?

According to Shakespeare, not much. You may well be familiar with the line in *Romeo and Juliet* when Juliet laments, 'What's in a name? That which we call a rose, by any word would smell as sweet.'

Yet, according to some brand strategists, it's the absolute make or break of a business.

I sit somewhere in between and know that there are millions of brands out there whose name has become synonymous with certain products or services, when at first glance it seems in no way related.

Apple?

Dell?

Mustard?

Old Spice?

Dove?

A brand name can often be where people stop their entire brand journey, as they become paralysed in the search for the absolute perfect word or coupling, which will somehow make the rest of the process simple. Neil Blumenthal admitted that he and his co-founders took six months to settle on the brand name Warby Parker and that it was one of the hardest things they did as a founding team. The name itself comes from two early Jack Kerouac characters Warby Pepper and Zagg Parker.

So, what really is in a name? And how do you decide on the right one for your brand?

Just like when you're choosing a name for a child, naming a brand can feel like an overwhelming task. Do you use our own name, such as Anya Hindmarch, Gorman or Paul Smith? Do you use an acronym that's easy to remember and spell but may need to be explained such as IBM, BMW or IKEA? Do you get clever and use something that actually means the opposite of what your brand is all about such as Slack (for workplace efficiency)? Do you try to evoke a feeling such as Virgin, Dove or Amazon? Or do you just make something up that sounds interesting and know you'll get to trademark it easily as it's not a 'proper' word such as Google, Qantas or Kodak?

Choosing from the top six

Most brand names fit into one (sometimes two) of the following six categories. (There are a few other categories for naming, but in my work I have found these six to be the most common and popular.)

	CATEGORY	DEFINITION	EXAMPLE
1	Descriptive	A functional or descriptive name that clearly states what the business/brand offers.	Whole Foods
2	Evocative	Evoking or suggesting something using words we associate with other meanings outside of the brand itself.	Dove
3	Invented	An experimental word that has been made up for the sake of the brand/business name.	Qantas
4	Acronymic	The use of an acronym to bypass having to spell out a long business/brand name.	IKEA
5	Founder's name	The use of a person's name, usually the founder or founders, or an historical figure that ties into the brand.	Louis Vuitton
6	Geographical	Utilising the region/location within a name to reflect on its origins or proximity.	Fiji Water

Business *to* Brand

Each of these categories has its pros and cons.

CATEGORY	PROS	CONS
Descriptive	Clear, succinct, describes easily what the brand delivers on. May initially help with things like Google searches and brand awareness due to functional nature.	Can be boring, not always able to stand out against competitors, may be harder to secure domains and social handles, can be restrictive if the brand offers change.
Evocative	Storytelling ability is good, usually elicits an emotional connection, more flexible than a descriptive/functional name.	Needs marketing to build associations, can be difficult to trademark, may not make sense based on products.
Invented	Can be easier to stand out and to trademark, score domains/social handles, etc. Can pique curiosity and works across all languages.	Needs marketing to build associations, challenging to remember and spell, lacks meaning and may be hard to pronounce.
Acronymic	Can be easier to remember, spell and trademark. May sometimes help with certain impressions, e.g. being more serious.	Often people have no idea what it actually stands for (IKEA, anyone?), can appear serious which may not suit brand personality.
Founder's name	May be uncommon which can be easier to trademark and secure online hubs, can humanise a brand, can help people connect to a name or family over a faceless entity.	Brand reputation hinders personal reputation. Can be harder to sell as you're attached to it. You may not have ownership over your own name legally in the future.
Geographical	Leverages the (potentially positive) identity traits of the location with your brand, may help in local brand awareness.	May restrict expansion, may be impacted by changes in government, natural disasters and other external forces.

Build with creativity

Consider the following questions when formulating your brand or rebrand name:

- Does your brand vision impact the category of brand name you choose? For example, if you're changing the way XYZ is done and setting a new narrative, an invented, totally original name may work well.

- Does it align with your business model and your revenue streams – current and future? (One of the reasons I changed my own brand name in my eighth year in business was that I felt it didn't align with my future revenue streams and business model.)

- Who is your chosen audience and are there certain emotions and words that will help them uncover and understand your brand in a way that perhaps another category would not?

- Do you intend to use a lot of storytelling and context creation of the name in your marketing and communications, or do you want a simple name that clearly states what you do?

- In terms of the outputs and how the brand will be communicated, especially through physical products, does the name need to be shorter or longer? For example, if you sell apparel, the brand name may need to be shorter to easily fit on a physical garment tag.

- How does your brand name work with others in the marketplace? (You should easily be able to research this given your work on positioning and competitive analysis.)

- What associations do you/your team/your friends, family and peers have with the name you have chosen? One way to check this is to set a stopwatch and write down as many word/phrase associations or meanings around the name you have chosen.

- How does the brand name tie into other brands/sub-brands you may have planned out?

- Could the brand name become passé in the near future, even if it is 'in' right now?

- Does the brand name refer to any popular culture reference, TV show or book that may become unknown or not in alignment with your audience in years to come?

- Is the brand name offensive or does it have any strange connotations in another language, particularly one in a territory you may be moving into? (Much has been made around the fact that ChatGPT, the AI tool, sounds like the French phrase *J'ai pété* which translates in English to 'I farted'. Add in 'Chat', which is the French word for cat, and you have the puzzling phrase, 'Cat, I have farted'.)

Business *to* Brand

- Will the brand name limit or restrict your expansion? (This can sometimes happen with service-based businesses that use their personal name then run into issues when hiring staff and having to relay to clients that it won't always be them that shows up to the meetings, despite the company being in their name.)

- Is the name easy to spell, find and pronounce? (As someone with an uncommon surname in the country I live in, I often have people avoid saying my name because they fear mispronouncing it and/or misspelling it in contracts, marketing collateral, etc.)

Once you have a shortlist of three to five of your top names, crosscheck that they not only appeal to you in the business, but also to your ideal audience. This is where word association activities, feedback groups and surveys can be helpful. With this point do remember that, just like with children's names, you don't have to take on board everyone's opinion and if you love it, stand by it.

You will also need to check if:

- the name is already in use by another business (locally as well as globally if you sell to both)

- the brand name is already registered by someone else, particularly within your industry

- the brand name, as an acronym, is offensive or spells something you wouldn't want associated with your brand

- associations of the word are just too difficult to get past.

These may seem like simple things but even people well versed in this space can come up against issues if they don't check them.

Case in point: years ago my friend Kate Dinon and I decided to put on some events. We were both experienced in branding and communications with over thirty years combined experience between us. Rushing to fill in an application for one particular festival, we put our initials together to create a 'name'. In our hastiness, we failed to notice what the initials of **F**iona **K**illackey and **K**ate **D**inon would spell. FKKD, anyone? While we were not trying to create a brand, and it didn't harm our application, it would have definitely helped if we had run through the checklist above.

You will also want to check things like social media handles; however, keep in mind that given how long social media has been around, it may not be possible to get the ideal handle. People today seem far more forgiving of social accounts whose handles include punctuation such as a period mark (.) or underscore (_).

Likewise, while it's great to be able to get a clean domain name (for example, mybrand.com), you may not be able to and it is becoming more common for businesses to choose a purposeful suffix that is not .com. In years prior we have seen a lot of tech start-ups choose a .co url, and more recently many younger brands or those aimed at gen Z have been utilising .xyz as their website suffix.

Trademarking is also something you may be doing at this stage, if you haven't already in your business journey. Trademark laws differ depending on the region/s you're covering but in most cases you can trademark a name, phrase, word, logo, picture, movement, sound, aspect of packaging, product/service name, and even smell – or any combination of those things. If you do choose to trademark, please get some professional advice. This can be a complex task and you may well easily miss something important if trying to DIY. While the cost can be high, it is worth doing to protect your brand now and into the future.

All of these things will impact the brand name you choose to go with or rebrand to. (I'll discuss my own journey with this in Chapter 11 when we cover rebranding.) Regardless of which avenue you go down, you absolutely must own it. You have chosen this name through consideration and effort and now it's time to stand behind it.

Lastly, remember that sometimes the brand name needs to grow on you. Just like parents who, in most cases, choose a name for their child before or very soon after they have even met them, a brand can develop into its name just as a child does until, at some point, you can't imagine it/them being called anything else. It just fits.

Brand story

The second part of this brand element relates to the story of your brand, from its origins through to how it operates today and its vision into the future. I grew up with Irish parents, whose heritage goes back on both sides for hundreds of years and both of my parents were incredible storytellers. But storytelling as an art isn't limited to any particular background or experience. Humans have relied on storytelling for millennia and while it can initially feel strange to do this in your business, sharing your own stories is instrumental in crafting a brand.

Imagine you are relaying the stories of your brand to someone who is five years old. How might you describe it? Now, how would you describe it to a thirteen-year-old? A fifty-year-old? What about an eighty-six-year-old?

In doing this simple exercise, you will begin to see common characters, traits and milestones. The language and tone may change but those things will stay the same. Keeping this in mind, consider your answers to the following questions. How might you use your answers to tell a story?

- What is the story of your own brand origins? Why and when did you start? Was there a catalyst or experience that moved you to finally begin?

- What were some of the funniest, most relatable stories about those early years? What makes you laugh looking back? How are you sharing this?

- Likewise, what's the story around your first hire? What was their story? How did they come to discover your brand? What attracted them most? Who are they as a person outside of work?

- When did you feel sad and stressed? What led to that? How did you move through those feelings?

- When did you feel at your absolute best and happiest in the business? What happened? Who else was there? How did you celebrate? How did you keep that feeling going?

We are all born storytellers. It's how we communicate our values, our beliefs and what we deem right and wrong. When it comes to brand you are telling the story of your vision, of your mission and beliefs, and doing so in a way that helps your audience not only understand why you started, but also where you're going and your purpose, and how they might see themselves reflected in those stories and connect with what you're creating.

Creativity: Personality and voice

Have you ever been on a bad date? Maybe it lasted an hour. (Maybe it's lasted a lifetime and you're somehow still on it – #Run!)

While there are any number of factors that contribute to a bad date, one of the most common is an absolute lack of personality. Dry, stilted conversation. Long, pregnant and awkward silences. Eyes failing to meet each other, your mind scraping around for something more interesting to think about, such as whether you put the laundry on or if you need more rinse in your dishwasher compartment.

The same situation can occur when we encounter businesses that have next to no personality. There is nothing to hold on to, nothing to pique our curiosity and not an ounce of creativity in sight.

So, what is a brand personality and how does it impact your brand voice?

Brand personality

The term 'brand personality' refers to the human traits or characteristics that a brand takes on (e.g. fun, quirky, sincere, strong, sweet, compassionate, friendly). We've all encountered brands that really feel like they have a strong personality, that feel almost human in some way, and it is this feeling that you want to evoke in your own brand.

Consider the work you have done on your vision, audience and brand archetypes. Now, consider the personality traits that help bring these all together. Are you an Outlaw brand that's super excited? Are you more of a Sage brand that's sophisticated? Are you an Innocent brand that's sweet and sincere?

Once you have an idea of your brand personality, it's time to test it using any one of these three activities:

1. The casting couch
2. The dinner guest
3. The amazing date

(There is no one perfect way to do this, so choose the one that feels the most creative for you. These are just some I've created that have worked well. If you want to come up with your own creative way to consider your brand personality and bring it to life, go right ahead.)

The casting agent

Imagine for a moment that you're in charge of casting the perfect person to play your brand in a film. Who would you be looking for? Would they be funny or serious? Upbeat or chilled? What might they be wearing that represents their usual attire? Would they be a loved character or would they be the cool, nonchalant one that people remember but never know the actual actor's name who played that role?

The dinner guest

Imagine your brand is turning up to an intimate dinner. There's a long table, beautifully decorated and people are beginning to enter the venue. Your brand walks in. Do they know everyone there and, if so, how do they greet them? A heartfelt hug? A double-cheek kiss? Air kisses? A solid handshake? A high-five? Do they not do any of these? What are they wearing? Who do they want to sit next to? What would their topics of conversation be?

The amazing date

Let's imagine you're playing Cupid and you're setting someone up on a date with your brand. What does your brand look like as a person? How do they show up? Do they arrive first and wait or are they the one coming in once everything has been set up? What is the typical first date your brand would go on? Is it a casual dinner or a fully organised extravaganza? If there's a film involved, what sort of film would it be? A big blockbuster? An arthouse foreign film that only one cinema is playing? A thought-provoking documentary on the state of XYZ? How would the date end?

These activities may seem a little fluffy at first, but having run them with numerous client groups I can tell you that once you start the conversation it's incredible to see the imagination, creativity and debate that comes up. Challenge and debate is exactly what you want in these circumstances so that everyone gets on the same page and you have one clear vision for the brand's personality.

You should now have a good understanding of the personality of your brand. From here you want to consider the brand messaging and voice you'll use to bring this personality to life, ensuring they fully align with your vision, mission and values.

Let's start with brand messaging.

Brand messaging

You could write an entire book about brand messaging (and many people have), but for the sake of space I'll aim to be succinct – which is apt, as brand messaging should also follow this rule.

Brand messaging refers to the way you communicate your brand's position, vision and value proposition in a clear and concise way. What is the number one promise you're making when people connect with your brand? What is the core message? What does everything you do, say and act out come back to? How can this be conveyed in a succinct way?

One way of succinctly showcasing your brand messaging is via a tagline (though know, as above, that messaging extends well beyond this).

In My Daily Business we use the tagline, 'Let's get you loving your business … on the daily'. Everything we do comes back to helping people enjoy their business and brand in a way that's consistent, not sporadic. Our offers and revenue streams all stem from answering the question: How can we make running a business and building a brand more enjoyable? How can we get people to consistently love what they do?

Here are some more brand examples:

- L'Oréal: Because you're worth it

- Toyota: Let's go places

- Nike: Just do it

- Airbnb: Belong anywhere.

Just like with brand names, this is where I find many people freeze; pressured to get the perfect tagline that becomes the next 'Just do it' instead of utilising the Nike sentiment to make a start.

Review the work you have done on your vision and mission, as well as your audience and positioning, and set a task to come up with thirty example taglines. Just knowing you have to create more than a couple will force you to get more creative and hopefully alleviate the pressure of one perfect sound bite on the first go.

One thing to keep in mind when coming up with your tagline or slogan is the use of emotive language and emotional drivers. According to Caroline Winnett and Andrew Pohlmann of the Nielsen Company, more than 90% of our purchase decisions are made subconsciously. Unfortunately, most small business owners focus only on the rational drivers of their brand within their communications (think: price, location, proximity, safety, durability) rather than the emotional – often subconscious – drivers (think: sex appeal, ambition, individuality, love, pleasure, giving back).

To create a strong brand, you must have a mix of rational and emotional drivers in your marketing and brand communications:

Rational driver + Emotional driver = Brand buy-in

In My Daily Business, the word 'love' is hugely emotive. Likewise, in all of the brand examples, emotive words and images are conjured: self-worth (L'Oréal), exploration (Toyota), ambition (Nike) and belonging (Airbnb).

How might you utilise emotive language and emotional drivers in your brand's core message? (For a free activity on this check out mydailybusiness.com/freestuff.)

Another task to try is the message architecture hierarchy (MAH).

This exercise is about making sure your messages are consistent, regardless of the connection channels you're using.

What happens to many brands is that they start off small with perhaps one or two people operating everything. Then as they gain momentum and financial success, the business grows and they hire people, eventually creating teams and departments. What often happens, however, is that the teams begin to form their own ideas about the brand's messages and essentially you end up with a business that is confusing its audience with its mixed messages.

This is where the message architecture hierarchy comes in. I first discovered this tool in the brilliant work of Margot Bloomstein, principal of Appropriate, Inc. and author of *Content Strategy at Work*, while I was working in the UK.

At the time I was heading up the marketing and content for the entire Amazon UK Kitchen and Home category, and I wanted to understand how my team could work on consistent messaging despite marketing a category that, at the time, boasted more than 8 million products. What were we trying to say? How could we streamline that?

When I later moved into a role as a brand content manager at a large accessories company, I used this framework again to look at how we could ensure that all of our teams (e.g. PR, digital, creative, retail, design) were speaking the same language. That our audience – regardless of which touchpoint they encountered – would know it was our brand by our consistent and clear messaging.

Many brands work without a message architecture hierarchy, with the brand's message being tweaked and changed depending on the department pushing it out (see below in Figure 6.3).

Figure 6.3. **Brand communication without message architecture hierarchy**

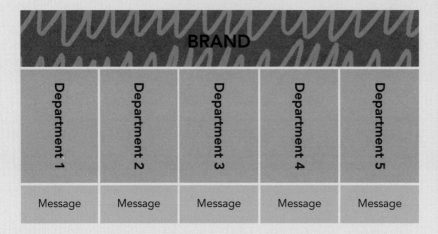

With Bloomstein's message architecture, the brand's messages are decided upon with all key stakeholders then shared with the entire company so that they remain consistent regardless of the department or marketing channel (Figure 6.4).

Figure 6.4 **Brand communication with message architecture hierarchy**

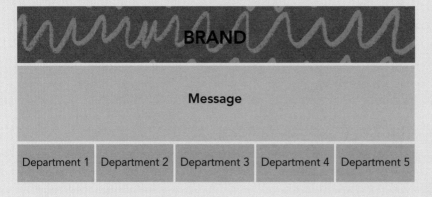

Build with creativity

While writing this book, I spoke with Margot about her framework.

'I developed the brand attributes exercise and BrandSort card deck to meet a few needs: while a team clarifies and prioritises their communication goals, they'll also build consensus and a shared vocabulary. Moreover, they'll have to make hard choices, saying yes to some ideas while leaving others behind. We can't communicate everything all the time, and this exercise makes tangible the effort of triaging our messaging. Each step supports those goals.

'First, the team will sort the cards into who they are, who they're not (qualities that better describe a competitor or just don't apply), and who they'd like to be. Then they can focus on just the current state and future state: what cards do they physically move over to carry into the future, knowing that some ideas they may want to leave behind in this deliberate evolution?

'Finally, they can review everything that's now in the future state column. They can organize the cards into thematic groups and they tell the story of those groups: what comes first? What's next? Document those decisions and the story and you've developed the message architecture.'

For example, you you may end up with a group of words in your 'future state' column that include:

- welcoming
- friendly
- fun
- approachable
- diverse.

You may decide that welcoming is the word that needs to come first and the one that best explains this group. So, you will have welcoming as your lead word, with diverse, friendly, fun and approachable as supporting words.

From a brand messaging point, this means you want to consider how to show 'welcoming' (not necessarily the word itself but what it represents) in all brand touch points (i.e. how are we truly showing up to be welcoming to people of all skin tones, ages, nationalities, religious beliefs, genders etc.)

Is this just the same as brand values?

No.

Message architecture differs in that it is actually a hierarchy unlike brand values which are, usually, all equally important.

For example, you might deduce from the exercise that the key messages your brand is aiming to be known for are:

- diverse

- empowering

- creative

- quality

- modern.

You would need to put them into a hierarchy. Which of these messages is *most* important for your brand to be known for? Which is the least important? If you could only express one of them via your next social media post, which one would you pick? You may also decide to list them according to priority.

For example:

1. diverse

2. empowering

3. quality

4. modern

5. creative.

(Think this exercise was a good one to help you define your brand's key messages? Then check out more of Bloomstein's work at Appropriate, Inc. – appropriateinc.com.)

Brand messaging can be hard and it is not something you necessarily land on in one afternoon. This is a stage in your brand journey where employing the help of a brand strategist and copywriter can be hugely effective and efficient.

Let's move on to brand voice.

Brand voice

We have just spent some time considering the human characteristics of your brand and your core brand message, and your brand voice needs to be in alignment with these.

Your brand voice is how you authentically and consistently express your brand in all channels and communications and connection points (not only externally but also internally – to employees, suppliers, stockists and manufacturers). This differs slightly to your brand tone of voice (which we will get into more detail soon), which is about the emotion and mood of your brand in different situations.

Earlier we discussed numerous psychological needs that we look for as humans. When it comes to your brand voice, being consistent across all mediums allows everyone interacting with the brand to feel a sense of trust as a result of pattern recognition. Just as we tend not to trust someone who seems to drastically change every time they're around new people, so too do we tend to distrust brands who do the same (e.g. the brand has one voice on social media and a completely different one in a physical location). An authentic brand is one that is consistent across all touchpoints, connection channels and communication efforts.

Consider your brand and the work you have done on its brand personality. Then consider the voice for your brand. What does it sound like?

Here are some words that may help:

- fun
- compassionate
- considerate
- reliable
- witty
- professional
- classic
- traditional
- upbeat
- positive
- cheeky
- down-to-earth.

Your brand voice dictates how you communicate and the overarching characteristics that make it consistent across all touchpoints.

Okay, let's talk tone.

Consider, for example, a good friend or family member you know really well. Think about how they talk, connect and present themselves in different scenarios. There will be commonalities between how they show up, regardless of who they are talking to or the situation they find themselves in. For example, they may always be friendly and funny.

Now, think of that family member or friend again and consider how their mood and tone may change depending on who they're talking to. They may still be friendly and funny in all situations, but their tone may be more relaxed and casual when talking to a friend vs a little more serious or reserved when talking to a work colleague or client. Their tone may differ but the overall voice is the same.

Your brand tone is the emotion, mood, word choice and communication style you use to convey your voice depending on the situation or channel. For example, you may have a brand voice that is warm, friendly, approachable and quick-witted. This is aligned with your brand personality and consistent across all touchpoints; however, you may adjust your tone to suit different environments (e.g. dialling up the wit on YouTube videos or increasing the friendliness level in your welcome email sequence or customer service communications).

Business *to* Brand

At this stage it's a good idea to start mapping out your brand's tone of voice document, which will help your brand communications to stay consistent. While there is no one way to create a tone of voice document, in my decades of experience in both creating and being the recipient of them, these are the most important elements to include:

- brand vision, mission, values and beliefs

- origin story

- audience profiles

- message architecture hierarchy

- words/phrases you don't use

- words/phrases you love to use

- grammatical notes (e.g. do you use slang?)

- examples of tone across different platforms (e.g. social, email, podcast, in-store, media, website)

- FAQs.

You can choose to create this as a digital PDF, or utilise a landing page on your website (unlinked if you wish for it to be non-public facing) for ease of updating.

When you feel confident in your brand personality and voice, it's time to look at bringing this (and everything else you have learned) to life visually.

Creativity: Visual identity

I can almost hear the exhale as you reach this part of the book.

Finally, we're getting to the good stuff!

Perhaps, you picked up this book thinking that this section – your brand's visual identity – would make up the bulk of its content. As you are now aware, your brand is SO MUCH MORE than simply your logo, typography choice and colour palette.

I have witnessed far too often small business owners running to create these elements without having done the foundational work. What ends up happening is that they either create something that looks exactly like everything else 'on trend' right now in their industry or they create something that needs to quickly be changed as the business grows and its founder realises how misaligned the visual identity is.

Don't let this be you.

Whether you are just starting out or decades in, the following tasks are useful in defining your visual identity.

Moodboarding

The first thing to do in defining your brand's visual identity is to start gathering inspiration through the use of moodboards. One of the best tools for doing this is Pinterest as you can keep these boards secret, add contributors and organise boards to have numerous folders. You can also try Milanote, but you'll need to upload more rather than using the search function like on Pinterest.

You'll want to create a moodboard for:

- overall vibe
- typography
- logo/sub-logos
- colour palette
- photography
- website
- emails
- social media
- ideal client.

And anything else you feel helps tell your brand story visually.

Understanding the requirements

The next step is to consider the type of brand collateral you'll need to have designed. Depending on your business, this might include digital assets (such as a website, emails, social media graphics and digital advertising) as well as print assets (everything from packaging and lookbooks, through to pull-up banners for events and care tags sewn into garments).

What are the visual requirements for your brand now and in the next three or five years? Are there categories you want to launch in the near future? Are there connection channels you're yet to use but hope to in future, such as a podcast (and therefore need to consider podcast artwork)? Do you have sub-brands to consider (ensuring your visuals don't come across jarring or inconsistent)?

Create a list of your brand collateral and start collating examples of each that speak to you. Again, you can use Pinterest or Milanote to house these so they can be easily shared with your team/designer.

Business *to* Brand

Creating a brand brief

The brand brief may be something you create only for yourself and your staff to come back to, or it may be something you choose to submit to various agencies or designers for initial quotes. If you're going down the latter path, I always recommend getting three quotes and seeing which feels right not only in terms of budget, but also compatibility between your brand and the person or business you'll be working with. Do you like their work? Are your values aligned? Do their other clients/portfolio work feel in line with your brand? Do they feel like a brand you'd be happy to work with again in the future?

Your designer's job is to get to the heart of what you're trying to achieve, so be as honest and transparent as possible with your likes, dislikes, objectives and overall vision.

I understand that at this stage you may decide to opt for a cheaper alternative by utilising sites such as Fiverr, Upwork and OnlineJobs.ph. If this is the case, make sure you are creating a relationship and paying appropriate remuneration for the task at hand. Remember that everything your brand does should be in alignment with who you say you are. And that you often get what you pay for.

In your brand brief, take all the work you have done to this point and create some sort of pack (a PDF is usually sufficient) that includes the following:

1. **Your brand vision, mission and values:** This can be simply shown on one page.

2. **Your target audience/s:** You may wish to share your buyer personas, Pinterest boards, customer feedback or anything else you feel will bring your audience to life for your designer/agency. You may also include links to your current clients/top customers or stockists. This will help your designer/agency to visualise the type of audience you're hoping to attract. If you don't yet have clients, customers or stockists, input your ideal customer (e.g. This is XYZ store in Portland which we would love to stock our products in).

3. **Your offers/product lines and services:** This is an outline of what you actually do. This might include all of the categories for product-based businesses or all of the services for service-based businesses. The designer/agency may well come up with some great additional items that can help with these products and services that you may have never considered before (e.g. recipe cards to insert with ceramic dishes you sell online, or stickers for sending gifts out, or tweaks that can make the packaging easier or which uses less plastic).

4. **Your bio or staff information:** It's important to share some of the humanity in your business, including information about the founders and staff who work there. It's great to add something they may not know yet, such as how you started the business (which could turn into inspiration for the designs) or that you love living by the ocean and you get your best ideas there (again, this may bring up ideas about colour and texture choice).

5. **Your mood boards:** Here you'll want to add in your overall brand feel, logo/s, typography (e.g. headline examples and body copy/normal text examples), colour palette, social media ideas (e.g. video thumbnails), photography and packaging (if applicable). Create one page per moodboard plus any additional

notes/text (e.g. 'This is a bit more youthful than we want to achieve but the colours are amazing – how could we make this more polished/sophisticated?'). If applicable, include anything else the designer/agency may need to know in relation to these things (e.g. 'The colour palette must align with our three sub-brands – colours and logos for these will be shared upon engaging chosen supplier'). (If you need help with this, we have a mini brand briefing course at mydailybusiness.com/courses and you can find links for tools like Milanote online.)

6. **Your requirements for design:** This is one of the key elements that often gets missed in initial conversations/briefings with designers/agencies, yet it is important to have the designer/agency mock up a design for an item that you will actually use (such as a podcast cover). So often a designer/agency may mock up a print business card when you might never use one. For this reason, it is important to list out all of the print and digital assets you will need created at this point in time (knowing it may change in the future). For example:

- Print assets: letterhead, envelope, lookbook template, tote bag
- Digital assets: social media templates, email signature, EDMs, website artwork, podcast cover art.

7. **Deliverables:** This is where you clearly state what you are looking for from the designer/agency in the brand visual identity. For example:

We are seeking a design studio/designer to work with us to create our visual brand identity. We have gone through a process of uncovering who the brand is, what we represent, the services/products we will offer and the people who will most delight in, and seek out, our creations. We are now looking for help bringing this to life in a visual format. This includes:

- logo
- typography
- colour palette
- a range of print and digital assets (as outlined in earlier pages).

We would like your quote to include costs for:

- 2–3 initial design/brand concepts
- 1 × full brand identity (as above, logo, typography, colour palette and assets)
- a digital style guide outlining looks and feel for all print and digital assets
- templates for these delivered in InDesign and Canva
- a full brand design guide
- website/eCommerce build (using a template in Squarespace/Shopify/Wix).

Please submit your quote no later than 10 am DATE, YEAR to me@mybrand.com

Business *to* Brand

You should have a few meetings with the designer/agency to dissect what concepts you love/dislike and be on the same page when it comes to the overall outcome, deliverables, deadlines and platforms for delivery (e.g. Adobe vs Canva).

Elements of design

Regardless of whether you are creating the visual identity yourself or working with someone else, you need to be aware of some of the most important elements of design.

Accessibility

A few years ago I worked with a disability-led arts organisation on the review of its brand strategy and communications plan. I was shocked to learn how few websites and other brand collateral is created with accessibility in mind – from colour combinations on websites which are incredibly difficult to read (even for a screen-reader machine), through to logo designs and collateral that is basically illegible. An example of a great and accessible brand design (at least at the time of writing this) is 1% for the Planet, which has partnered with Accessible Web's A11Y program to ensure that they have created an easily accessible website. You can input your own website and check its accessibility rating at accessibleweb.com/website-accessibility-checker.

Trademarking

As discussed in Chapter 2 when we looked at the brief history of brand, and again in this chapter when we looked at brand naming, trademarking is an important element of protecting your brand, particularly its visual brand identity. It won't always prevent other companies from trying to 'pass off' their product or service as somehow related or associated with your brand, but it can do a lot to deter this from happening. Seek legal counsel to ensure you know exactly which trademarks are applicable to your brand in which territories and that these are sought correctly. When it comes to design you want to ensure you're not putting your brand in danger of litigation or copycat claims.

Positioning

At this stage you want to ensure your visual identity matches the positioning work you have already done. One of the quickest ways to lose trust is to have a mismatch between how a brand believes itself to be perceived and how it actually is perceived, through poor execution of a visual identity. I am still shocked to see people from well-known brands that have incredible visuals on their socials and website utilise dated clip art when presenting at an event or during a masterclass. Stay consistent and ensure the way you wish to be perceived is visually represented at every touchpoint.

Colour psychology

Back in Chapter 2 we looked at the way psychology marries into brand. One of the biggest ways to do this visually is to utilise colour psychology when planning out your colour palette.

One place to start when coming up with, or refreshing, a colour palette for your brand is with a psychology of colour chart (see Figure 6.5 on page 164). The colour wheel is not a new concept, and its origins date back to the 1600s with Sir Isaac Newton and the 1700s when Johann Wolfgang Goethe began looking at the way in which colour impacts psychology.

Colour can have a huge impact on how we feel about a brand. For example, if your brand is bold, vivacious and outgoing, it may not feel in alignment with a monochromatic colour palette. Likewise, if your brand is in the children's health space, it may make more sense to have a more colourful and bright palette rather than a neutral one, to help kids feel great when visiting your locations or coming into contact with your products.

Figure 6.5 **The psychology of colour chart**

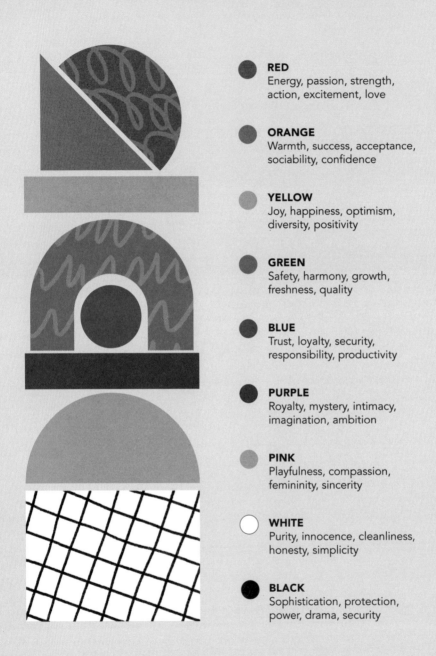

RED
Energy, passion, strength, action, excitement, love

ORANGE
Warmth, success, acceptance, sociability, confidence

YELLOW
Joy, happiness, optimism, diversity, positivity

GREEN
Safety, harmony, growth, freshness, quality

BLUE
Trust, loyalty, security, responsibility, productivity

PURPLE
Royalty, mystery, intimacy, imagination, ambition

PINK
Playfulness, compassion, femininity, sincerity

WHITE
Purity, innocence, cleanliness, honesty, simplicity

BLACK
Sophistication, protection, power, drama, security

Build with creativity

Considering what you know about your brand's archetypes, personality and voice, which colours really reflect what you're creating? How will they be part of the visual language you use?

What should you end up with?

By the end of the visual branding process, a decent designer or agency should be able to deliver the following documents to help you not only launch but also show up consistently with your visual brand identity. These will usually come as a result of the designer initially showing you three concepts, of which you will pick one to continue with. You will want to have a way of easily accessing these documents, to amend and tweak for new marketing channels.

1. **Brand style guide:** This is an absolute must and will include everything from your typography (e.g. font names and style, bold/italics, heading/body fonts) and colour palette (including RGB and HEX numbers for each tone), to your photography styling and mock-ups of key channel graphics (e.g. email templates), and information on how to use/not use logos, type and colours (primary vs secondary).

2. **Brand templates:** The amount of templates will depend on your budget and who you are working with. Templates may include social media graphics (e.g. templates for Instagram grid, reels, stories, TikTok covers), emails (e.g. status, broadcast, sale), flyers and packaging (see Figure 6.6 on page 166). Many designers will choose to deliver these templates in an Adobe tool (such as InDesign or Illustrator), but more and more nowadays these are being delivered in drag-and-drop design tools such as Canva, which can be easier for some people to use (especially those without design knowledge).

3. **Brand mentoring:** Again, this will depend on your budget and who you are working with, but many designers/agencies will offer ongoing mentoring or retainer packages where they can update graphics and design elements on a monthly or quarterly basis. This may come in handy for seasonal campaigns (e.g. Mother's Day) and/or things you wish to support (such as a cause or notable key date that's relevant to your industry).

In the list above, a brand style guide and templates are basic minimums. An agency or designer who is not able to deliver these is not someone you want to work with #HarshButTrue. Showing up consistently is part of what builds trust with a brand and you'll need a brand style guide and templates in order to do this.

Once you have all of this you'll need to schedule in time and set a deadline for full implementation of the new brand collateral across all mediums and channels.

Business *to* Brand

Figure 6.6 **Example social media templates by brand agency New Opening Studio**

Image: newopening.studio

Creativity: Content

How will you utilise content, in all its mediums, to connect with your audience, cut through the noise and cultivate a genuine community?

At the heart of all content creation is the desire to connect. We may choose to do that through humour, education, inspiration, heartfelt human stories, news updates and even controversy. Given the plethora of ever-expanding channels and platforms and ways to connect through content, how do you decide on the topics you'll talk about and the themes you want your brand to be known for?

One simple way is to figure out your content pillars.

When it comes to content, curiosity is your greatest asset. When you can pique someone's curiosity you have their attention and, in this day and age, attention is a currency that brands need to be conscious of.

One simple framework that works well regardless of the size of your brand is to consider how to support your content strategy with key content messages and pillars. These are the key themes you want to be the go-to brand for. Without knowing these, you'll get sucked into thinking you need to start on each platform and channel from scratch (which is a distribution-first mindset and almost always leads to inefficiencies internally as well as confusion externally).

If you have a marketing/creative team or contractors, get them involved with this exercise. But it's also fine to do solo if you're the main decision-maker and creative in your business.

1.   Get out a blank piece of paper, a new digital document or a clean whiteboard.

2.   Write down your brand's core message in the middle. Then consider everything that comes up for your audience around this message. For example, if I wrote down 'Let's get you loving your business … on the daily', I might then consider all the reasons people don't love their business such as stress, anxiety, overwhelm, money challenges, time management, procrastination and boredom.

3.   Next, do the same again but with the main industry you're in (e.g. for My Daily Business it would be business education) and consider your audience's interests in this space. For example, it may be passive income, money, wealth creation, systems, technology, freedom, time back, digital nomad, public speaking, brand ambassadors, sustainability, ethical supply chains, productivity, mindfulness, creativity, studio design, cash flow, and so on.

4.   Which words/phrases can you group together? For example, I could put mindfulness, stress, overwhelm, anxiety, procrastination and boredom all under the theme 'mindset'. Keep going until you have around five to seven group themes.

5. Cull the least important ones so that you end up with four themes.

6. Add your brand in so that you now have five themes. For example, for our brand we have mindset, money, systems and processes, brand and marketing, and My Daily Business. These are all the things we want to be known for.

When you have these themes and feel that they align with your overall brand vision, consider how they reflect your positioning. Do they stand out? If they are similar to others in your industry, how might your personality and tone of voice help attract, engage and retain your audience? You may wish to go back through your work on competition and positioning to check that they work.

You can also use your content pillars to help find strategic marketing ideas that are also SEO-friendly. An example of this might be when you have a content pillar such as money and input this into a search engine, such as Google. Once a search results page loads, you can then scroll down and see what other questions people may have asked about 'money', such as 'How can I make more money?', 'How much money should I have?' and 'What are the four types of money?'. You may then wish to use these as content ideas for your brand, knowing that they are a) popular questions and b) linking back to what you want to be the go-to brand for.

In the next chapter we will look at how you can bring these to life after selecting your key marketing channels and platforms and how you can plan, batch and create content consistently for an authentic brand voice that instils trust.

TASKS TO CONSIDER

This has been another chunky chapter with loads to consider when it comes to the creativity behind your authentic brand.

Work through the following tasks or download them in a worksheet form online via the QR code below.

1. *Using the knowledge you have gained so far, work through the tasks for each of the creativity elements:*

    *   *positioning*
    *   *competition*
    *   *name and story*
    *   *personality and voice*
    *   *visual identity*
    *   *content.*

2. *Revisit your answers in Figure 3.5 (page 62) and look at how you originally ranked these six elements for your brand.*

3. *Now that you have done the work (or come back to this when you have), where would you rank yourself now?*

4. *How has this ranking changed? What further changes are necessary?*

5. *When will you take action on these? Get out the calendar and schedule this in.*

Before we get stuck into Chapter 7 we will hear from Mark Adams, the Managing Director of Vitsœ. As you'll quickly see, Mark has quite a different perspective on the term 'brand' to me. I chose to include this interview as Vitsœ is a brilliant company and Mark has been its Managing Director since 1993. He is an incredible force for change and someone I deeply respect. I also wanted to include it as a real-life example of how terms can mean different things to different people. I would like to think Mark and I are both coming at this from the same perspective: create good businesses and ensure people feel a connection to them so that together you can do more good in the world.

(You can find out a bit more about Mark in the fabulous documentary *RAMs* (2018), available at hustwit.com/rams.)

 Scan for digital worksheet

Business *to* Brand

Image: ©Vitsœ

Profile: *Vitsœ*

For more than half a century Vitsœ has been helping people enjoy simple, well-designed furniture pieces that are built to last. In 1959, founder Niels Vitsœ alongside Otto Zapf established the company to bring to life the furniture designs of Dieter Rams – one of the foremost industrial designers of the twentieth century. Dedicated to creating pieces that last and have less impact on the environment, Vitsœ has become an example of what's possible when you focus on fully aligning business activity and vision.

'Vitsœ is the result of sixty plus years of hard graft: allowing more people to live better, with less, that lasts longer.'

Since 1993 Mark Adams has been Vitsœ's Managing Director. Here's his view on the concept of brand and his insights into why Vitsœ has remained so successful more than sixty years after its creation.

If you had to sum up Vitsœ the brand in one sentence, what would it be?

The word 'brand' is not allowed at Vitsœ. A brand is a hot piece of metal applied to an unfortunate cow's backside. It is a sign of ownership; it is imposed from the outside. Branding consultancies have adopted it in precisely that manner: an artificial construct to impose upon a can of fizzy sugar or similar. Vitsœ is Vitsœ. Vitsœ is not a brand. Vitsœ is the result of sixty plus years of hard graft: allowing more people to live better, with less, that lasts longer.

What do you believe is the difference between running a business and being the custodian of a brand?

Everyone who works at Vitsœ is the custodian of Vitsœ, not a brand.

Few brands have been able to remain as consistent – and successfully so – as Vitsœ. Why do you think this is?

The answer is implicit in your question: most brands are an artificial construct, hence they are rarely as consistent as Vitsœ. Outsiders observe integrity and authenticity at Vitsœ. It starts with Vitsœ's notoriously rigorous recruitment process: only those who genuinely wish to make a difference to our troubled planet will successfully join the team at Vitsœ. And, of course, the second that a company accepts outside investment from angels or private equity, that's the moment it dies. Vitsœ has never accepted the many offers from external investors.

Every single touchpoint at Vitsœ seems so aligned with who the brand is, from the initial response to an email enquiry through to the care and attention given to potential buyers through to the way the items are packed. The brand experience is impeccable. How does this actually happen in terms of onboarding staff, training, design, systems?

How much time do you have? Here is the short answer ... Vitsœ sees the recruitment process as a two-way conversation giving the opportunity to candidates to make an informed decision on whether Vitsœ is a place of work for them. This requires listening to candidates and being open about Vitsœ's practices. The purpose of the process is to develop teams of like-minded people sharing the same values. Firstly, Vitsœ looks for characters who will fit in its community; skills come second. This approach allows people from unusual and diverse backgrounds to thrive at Vitsœ.

Vitsœ's recruitment process is acknowledged as thorough. It starts with the insistence on a covering letter; followed by a phone call in which the candidate cannot be seen, intentionally; only then might a face-to-face interview be granted, at which a candidate is asked to bring something that they have made. The final step is a discovery day where the candidate has the opportunity to meet potential future colleagues and discover much more about Vitsœ. At the end of that day up to a dozen colleagues stand in a circle to assess the candidate before an offer is made. Everybody's voice is equal.

Once a candidate joins Vitsœ – and becomes a colleague to everyone else – there is an induction period of a few weeks in which the new colleague travels around the business to work with people in many different teams. International recruits will live in the residential accommodation in Vitsœ's production building, becoming fully familiar with their colleagues and the way of working before being let loose on customers in Vitsœ's international shops.

A quote from Annie, a Vitsœ colleague, is: 'We are all so different, but it really works. You need a mix of personalities and I think it's great that there are people from all sorts of backgrounds because that's what rounds out the team.'

Vitsœ's team of eighty-five is looked after by a professional facilitator, and a people and culture person. In-depth reviews are regular, friendly and constructive. Vitsœ's recruitment process was featured in a *Harvard Business Review* article, 'Hire Slow, Fire Fast' by Greg McKeown.

Vitsœ is a brand that is so recognised and respected, yet somehow still understated. How has the brand been able to ride the wave of success without losing its roots or becoming so mainstream as to lose its edge?

It's a perceptive question, one that we can read by removing the word 'brand', twice. The answer is: single-mindedness, or bloody-mindedness. Ruthless commitment to the cause. Constantly, politely saying 'No' to the pressure for new products, 'brand extension', or outside investment. Therefore resisting every temptation to chase selfishness and greed – brands call it 'growth' – at the expense of staying utterly true to one's purpose: allowing more people to live better, with less, that lasts longer.

Vitsœ has been able to really cultivate a community of loyal fans around it, helping to advocate for the brand and being its greatest ambassadors. What do you put that down to?

Customers can smell authenticity, just as much as they can smell selfishness and greed. They can see that Vitsœ charges everyone the same price, irrespective of who they are; that there are no sales, no discounts or commission earned. They can see that everyone wants to work at Vitsœ. They can see that everyone has a genuine interest in the long-term relationship, not the quick buck.

What do you think the biggest myth is around the idea of building a brand today?

Er, the concept of the brand as an inauthentic artificial growth-driven construct. Now with extra greenwashing added for good measure. (You will not find the word 'sustainable' on Vitsœ's website, except when used by external writers.)

How has the vision for the company changed over time, or has it remained the same now as it was at the beginning?

The trick is to leave no stone unturned while establishing one's purpose as a company. Then to stick ruthlessly to that purpose each and every day. But to be able to change radically one's vision while being consistent with that purpose. Vitsœ was an early adopter – late 1990s – of what has become known as D2C, direct-to-consumer. Vitsœ is a dotcom, selling directly to customers in ninety countries. But Vitsœ is still Vitsœ.

Niels Vitsœ, the founder of Vitsœ, passed away in 1995. How has the brand been able to continue his vision and how do you assess this as the brand has grown and expanded?

Authenticity: Niels Vitsœ did not pass away in 1995; he died. Mark Adams was fortunate enough to spend ten years with him before his death, and so far to have spent almost forty years working with Dieter Rams. That absorption process has allowed the distilled essence of Vitsœ to be passed on to the next generations. Vitsœ is currently in advanced planning for the evolution of the ownership of the company for those generations, creating a model that will suit the subtle beast that is Vitsœ.

What's the best brand advice you have ever received and why did it leave such an impact?

To have worked out how inauthentic the concept of a brand is. Do not be a brand. Understand your purpose. Be yourself. Be authentic.

Why do you think building a brand, and not simply a business, is important today?

The question is entirely flawed. Vitsœ is a company. The origin of 'company' is 'cum pane', 'with bread': the situation in which bread was broken and decisions were taken. The evolution from those groups became known as a company. And the folk were companions (note the origin of that word, too). You need to build an authentic altruistic company, not a growth-driven, selfish ... brand.

These words were written by Mark Adams, without the editing of colleagues who normally prefer to soften his tone of voice.

Web: vitsoe.com

IG: @vitsoe

TT: @vitsoeofficial

Image: ©Vitsœ

Business *to* Brand

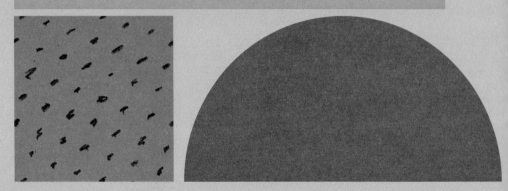

07.

Focus on elevation

My husband and I chose to have our first child while living in London, despite all of our family living on the other side of the world, approximately 17,000 kilometres away. To fill the geographical gap, I would phone my mum and my sister most mornings on my way to work, and when my pregnancy got further along I would call them more often, asking for their advice and counsel. They were pretty amazing at it which would make sense given my sister is a regional GP who specialises in obstetrics and gynaecology and my mum worked for decades as a midwife and registered nurse.

On one particular phone call back home, my sister interrupted my ramblings about my child's impending birth with words I'll never forget. 'Fiona, remember the preparation for the birth is great but the birth is just the very first day of being a parent and parenthood is a club you'll be part of for life. The most important work you'll do is showing up every day AFTER that child is born, as the best parent you can possibly be. That's when things get real.'

Understanding your brand's vision, mission and values, its audience, positioning and place in the market are all absolutely essential to creating a transformative brand, but the real – and often harder – work is bringing that all to life in a way that elevates your brand in the minds of your chosen audience to become their go-to option today, tomorrow and into the future.

It's time to get elevated.

In the ACE brand model, elevation is about bringing everything together in a way that is in full alignment with your vision, values and positioning. It is about cementing what you believe in and infiltrating that in every part of the business, from onboarding of staff through to the connection channels you choose to utilise. It is about staying true to your core and building brand authority, creating systems that enable future opportunities while being aware of possible threats and adapting to reduce negative outcomes. An elevated brand is also one that uses technology and other data points to measure, analyse and improve its impact, and to ensure that impact. Most of all, an elevated brand is one that is absolutely diligent in its focus on genuine alignment to purpose and staying true to its promise.

The elevation in the ACE brand model includes a brand's:

1. connection channels

2. people

3. authority building

4. future thinking

5. analytics and impact

6. alignment.

Let's get into them.

Focus on elevation

Elevation: Connection channels

When I started out in the brand and marketing space it was 2001. While the internet was around, social media and smartphones were not. In the space of two decades, the ways in which brands can not only communicate to, but also *with*, their audiences has bypassed anything we could have imagined.

If you have ever watched the original 1984 version of *Gremlins*, you may well remember the rapid and scary multiplication of these seemingly cute and harmless creatures. For many business owners the sheer volume of marketing channels and the speed at which they seem to multiply can feel just as terrifying. Everywhere you look it seems another marketing channel has popped up and you're suddenly wondering a) if your brand needs to be on it and b) if so, what you're even supposed to be saying.

So, how do you decide on the best connection channels for your brand? Part of the answer is held within the question. Where are the best places to genuinely *connect*, not just simply show up and add to the noise?

Review the work you have done on your audience/s so you fully understand who they are and what they need from your connection channels. Why would they want to connect? What would keep them coming back and bringing others with them?

Also consider your values, revenue streams and business model, as well as the overall brand goals you have set. How will different connection channels feed into achieving these? For example, if one of your values is 'education' and one of your key revenue streams is consulting packages, it may make sense to give your audience a taste of what they would be in for by choosing a connection channel like podcasting or YouTube. Likewise, if one of your values is 'connection' then the channels which elicit that in person, such as events, keynotes and retreats, may work best to bring that value to life as well as feed into your business model and revenue streams.

As someone who studied journalism and also worked as a journalist for more than twenty years, I often opt to put every question that comes up in business through the Five W's test: Who? What? When? Where? Why? This also works in choosing your brand connection channels.

The five Ws

When it comes to connection points, the first thing you must be clear on (and you should be now thanks to the tasks in Chapter 5) is who you're trying to connect with and why they would be searching for what your brand offers. Take this knowledge and work through the Five Ws.

Who?

Who are you trying to connect with? Who is in their circle of influence (e.g. media, friends, influencers, news companies)? Who do they need social proof from in order to trust your brand?

What?

What type of content will they best connect with? What mediums do they prefer (e.g. longer-form video tutorials or short bite-size audio podcasts)? What do they need to know about your brand and what is the best medium to deliver this message before they engage with your products or services? What words and phrases might they use to search and on what platforms? What is your budget?

When?

When will they most likely connect with your brand? (For example, we have been sending a Sunday night email to thousands of small business owners for years, as this is a time when many have the mental space to learn, read and reflect. Many of our subscribers say they open it first thing Monday morning as a way to pep themselves up before a work week commences. You can join it yourself at mydailybusiness.com/subscribe.) When are they looking for what it is you sell? When will they move from being interested to converting? When will they become advocates?

Where?

Where are they most likely to form genuine connections? (For example, a podcast or evening Zoom workshop may work better for parents of school-aged children who may not be able to make a live 8.30 am event.) Where do they hang out online and IRL? Where is their circle of influence? Where might they be most seeking what it is your brand offers?

Why?

Why will selecting this connection channel help in bringing your vision to life for your audience? Why will this channel help guide them through the buyer cycle from awareness to advocacy? Why would they see value in this channel and your brand content? Why is this going to help them in some way?

Focus on elevation

Starting the *My Daily Business* podcast as a key connection channel came as a direct result of running through the Five W's exercise. While our Sunday email has worked well, we knew we needed another channel that could be binged by people new to our brand, as well as be a trusted source of inspiration, motivation and education for loyal listeners who might have us on while packing orders, creating pieces, commuting between sites and taxiing family members around to various activities.

One thing to point out here is that your key connection channels should start with platforms wherein you have some ownership, such as a podcast, vlog, blog and/or email. Social media is a fantastic connection channel, especially for distributing content and analysing its impact with your audience, but it is not something you own. Too often I see small business owners attempt to build brands using only social media, with next to no other connection channels, which then fall apart when the platform changes its algorithm or when they lose their audience and/or their account gets hacked.

If it helps, you may like to consider the acronym CORE content, which means to Create Once, Repurpose Everywhere. That is, create valuable content using one core channel such as a podcast and then repurpose that podcast content across multiple channels such as a blog (transcription or text format of the podcast episode), vlog (video recording or snippets of the podcast episode) and social media (video snippets as TikToks, YouTube Shorts and IG Reels, quotes as quote cards and key takeaways as five-slide carousel posts). Again, your CORE content channel should be a platform where you have some ownership, and not a social media platform for the reasons just mentioned.

Choosing your frequency of connection

Once you have chosen your connection channels, decide on how often you'll show up as a brand and, well, *connect*. This is your week-in, week-out content that will bring your brand to life, staying front of mind for your audience and enabling anyone travelling through the buyer cycle to be guided to the next stage.

For example, you may have chosen email marketing as a key connection channel. How often will you send an email? Will you send various types (e.g. a weekly 'tips and links' style broadcast and another email for paid members who wish to dive deeper into your brand's communication)? If you have a particular social media platform as part of your connection channel mix, how often will you show up? Remember this isn't about being on every channel 24/7 but about showing up in a way that aligns with your values and beliefs and ensures your brand's message is getting out there. When considering the buyer cycle, which channels will help guide people in their research of your brand? Which channels will help the post-purchase connections lead to advocacy?

As you may have guessed by now, I'm someone who likes to map things out visually, and one way I've discovered to do this for myself and my clients is via a basic BAU (Business-as-Usual) content matrix (below in Figure 7.1).

Figure 7.1 **BAU content matrix**

DAILY	WEEKLY	FORTNIGHTLY	MONTHLY
• IG Stories x 2 • TT x 1	• IG Grid x 2 • IG Reel x 3 • Paid Email • YT Re-purpose • Podcast x 1	• Broadcast Email • PI Updates • LI Article x 1	• Pitch Media / Other Podcasts x 4 • Retention Email

QUARTERLY	BI-ANNUAL	ANNUAL
• Media x 1 • Hit Podcast x 2 • Webinar x 1 • Audit POS materials	• Social Audit • Website Audit • Figurehead Audit	• EOY Live Event

Now, this may look a little overwhelming, particularly if you have a small brand with minimal resources; however, keep in mind that there is no perfect number of posts, emails and podcast episodes that will help bring every brand to life. You could have one or two channels and do them really well, or you could have ten. You must decide on which connection channels you will use and how often you will choose to connect. Remember, consistency helps build trust. If you can only commit to sending a quality email every quarter then start there rather than promising your audience that you'll send an email every week and giving up after four to five weeks.

Brand alignment is also key. If you are a brand that's all about slow living and calming the senses, then it may not feel right to be sending out twenty-four screaming videos a day on TikTok or twenty-one emails over seven days as part of your welcome sequence.

The next stage is to work backwards and figure out what this means on a monthly and annual basis. For example, if you are putting out one podcast episode a week, you'll have roughly fifty-two in the year and four to five per month. This is where your content pillars come in. So if you have five pillars and fifty-two podcast episodes, that's roughly ten times the episodes per pillar (with two episodes left over). You can then decide on the topics of those ten episodes under that one pillar and schedule in when you'll create them. This ensures your brand content will always come back to what you want to be known for and that you're not simply adding ad-hoc and scattergun content into the mix of endless noise that's already out there.

It should really go without saying that content and connection must be authentically aligned with your brand's values and beliefs, goals, voice and personality to genuinely create a connection. Too often I see people live by some arbitrary rule that they must show up 1257 times a week on social media to grow a brand. This is simply not true and countless brands have proven that slow and steady can win people's trust over crappy, high-quantity content.

Elevation: People

It's often said that 'people are your greatest asset' and when creating an elevated brand it's your people that are going to help maintain that elevation. How are you choosing people who genuinely and authentically want to work with your particular brand? How will you ensure that the actions of your staff are aligned with your brand's vision and values? This can feel a lot easier to do when your brand is small and is something that many bigger brands begin to lose focus on or control of as they grow.

Here are the key elements you need to ensure that you'll not only attract great people, but also retain them.

1. **Be clear across all touchpoints as to what your brand is all about:** Be clear to anyone even remotely connecting with the brand about your vision, values and overall purpose and mission. This is the very first starting point in attracting people who genuinely want to be part of what it is you're seeking to achieve. If a potential candidate were to google your brand, what would come up? Likewise, if they reviewed the 'About' or 'Our Story' section of your website, is there sufficient information to help them know why it was started and what it might be like to work with your brand?

2. **Invest in a thorough recruitment process:** This means that you genuinely consider the process through which you'll not only assess whether a candidate is right for the job but also that your brand is the right fit for them. Prior to starting my own business I worked in senior roles for some of the largest companies in the UK and Australia. What I witnessed were incredibly different ways of recruiting, many of which followed a basic model that gave little chance for the candidate to understand what they were getting into, or for the brand to really understand the different perspectives of the candidate's character. Amazon – for all its flaws – has, in my personal experience working in its UK HQ, an amazing and intensive recruitment process for the marketing roles. This consisted of two examinations, a phone call and then a full assessment day that featured quizzes, role playing, creative ideation and campaign planning. An entire team of people would assess each candidate who would meet with a full spectrum of potential colleagues to really get a sense of the work involved and the pace at which it was to be executed.

3. **Don't be afraid to think differently:** It's an interesting thing to observe how quickly so many brands and businesses have come to adapt to changing technologies, new platforms and marketing channels, and yet how few have changed up the way they recruit, onboard and review their staff. I work with many CEOs and MDs of large companies who have hired for executive and senior roles (with correspondingly high expectations and pay ranges) but have never asked the candidate for anything 'extra' such as an audit of their brand and what they might change with a million-dollar budget, or for a 10-10-10 presentation (what we should be changing within 10 minutes, 10 months and 10 years as a company). In so many companies, staff are given a minimal onboarding period with little more than a 'check the intranet' in terms of the brand's DNA, company culture and processes. And when it comes to reviews,

staff are asked to prepare their own self-assessment and then graded on how well they do against often unrealistic expectations. In so many ways, the humanity appears to have been taken out of the entire process and yet it is the humanity and purpose behind a brand that leads to greater staff satisfaction, engagement and retention. How might you utilise your brand's vision, values and personality to make the recruitment, onboarding and review processes more aligned? For example, if you have a 'fun' and 'upbeat' brand personality, how does that come across in the way your staff engage with the business from their initial job application through to their biannual review?

4. **Set them up for success:** One of my first questions to clients who relay experiences of poor staff engagement or a misalignment is: have you set them up for success? That is, are they absolutely clear on how they fit into the greater brand? Do they know the value their role brings to the company? Which piece of the puzzle are they in charge of? Do they have the systems and processes set up to be able to not only do their job but also excel at it and get curious about how it – and the brand at large – might be improved? Are they given the opportunity for input or do internal politics and hierarchy stifle their creativity? How might you put in place systems for success when it comes to the people working within your brand? How are you aligning your brand vision and values with your people management?

5. **Nurture the relationship:** Just as any long-term relationship, be it romantic or platonic, needs nurturing, so too does the relationship between your brand and its people. In 2015 I visited the New York HQ of Warby Parker, where big blue numerical balloons – highlighting the number of years someone has been employed there – adorned the backs of chairs and staff were encouraged to have a quiet moment in the hidden library or get together in a variety of creative and fun ways. As the brand's founders showed us around, it was obvious they not only knew their staff but also had genuine relationships with them, checking in on family members, cracking jokes and asking how people felt about certain projects. Jeff Bezos famously stated that your brand is what others say about you when you have left the room and there's no greater check on a company's culture than when staff are asked – at a random barbecue or when meeting someone new – what it's like to work at XYZ brand. Whatever comes out of their mouth is the direct result of your ability to nurture – or not.

6. **Open up opportunities:** Hand in hand with nurturing relationships is enabling your staff to seek out opportunities and test experiences within the brand. For example, you might have someone in the retail team who would love to transfer into the design team, or there might be someone in accounts who has a brilliant eye for photography and who would love the chance to test it out in a social media shoot. Too often brands don't look within when seeking to fill a role, having placed their staff into boxes that can feel restrictive. Could your brand host an expo day/week where anyone who wants to can spend time in another team, seeing what they do and testing if it might be an area they'd like to move into?

There are many other ways to get the best out of your staff and create genuine brand ambassadors within the company, but these elements should help get your creative ideas flowing about what's possible.

Elevation: Authority building

If you have ever had to hire someone, you'll know what a difficult task it can be. After all, people can appear however they like on paper and, to a lesser degree, in interviews. It's usually only after you have started working with them that you can begin to see if they measure up to what you had imagined. One of the tactics recruiters and hiring managers use to calculate if a candidate is right for the job is to get references – that is someone else's opinion on the candidate's skillset, initiative and overall abilities.

In the same way, your audience will often look for your brand's authority through who the brand is associated with. For example, in the case of allied health, this may be certain bodies and institutions, while for a lighting designer it may be through recognition in the way of awards and media features.

As much as you may wish to rally against this, it's a fact that we are social animals and we often rely on social proof to validate our assumptions. This social proof can help in resurrecting brand loyalty from past clients and customers as well as attracting a new audience.

So, how do we cultivate it and build our brand authority? Here are four ways that I've found to be the most effective for my clients.

1. **Collaborations:** Humans have been collaborating since time began and yet, for some reason, many brands shun the idea of joining forces for a common goal. Collaboration can be an incredible opportunity to connect with another brand's audience and introduce yours to them in a way that is mutually beneficial. Collaborations may be as simple as a one-off low-key marketing campaign through to a fully-fledged long-term partnership. For collaborations to be successful, they must be a win-win for both parties and be in alignment with your brand's vision, mission and values.

2. **Awards and industry recognition:** As someone with a background in journalism, I understand both the cynicism that can exist when it comes to awards and the opportunities that the recipient, or finalist, of an award can gain in terms of brand awareness, connections and credibility. When it comes to building your brand authority in an authentic way, do some research into the awards that are most meaningful to your audience/s as well as those that align with your own vision and values.

3. **Accreditations:** Much like awards, these can elicit both negative and positive responses, and yet if you review your brand goals, vision and positioning, you may decide to be accredited with various institutions and key bodies. Some of these will be absolutely essential (such as a psychology brand being accredited with the local psychological association), whereas others may be down to your understanding of what is most important to your audience. For brands that are aiming to position themselves as ethical and sustainable, a B-Corp accreditation or 1% for the Planet membership may be the thing that sets them apart from their competition.

4. **Figurehead marketing:** This is about building the awareness of your brand's figurehead, which may well be you as its founder, a CEO, managing director or creative director. Not only does this humanise your brand by bringing your people to the forefront, but it also allows for the brand's elevation to happen through the wisdom, humanity and storytelling of its figurehead. This may present as everything from panel discussions, books and keynote speeches, through to a content series, podcast and opinion pieces, cementing your figurehead – and consequently the brand – as an expert in their field.

After reviewing the different ways to build brand authority, write down five to ten ideas to begin the process of making this happen for your own brand.

Business *to* Brand

Elevation: Future thinking

In Chapter 5 we looked at your brand architecture, thinking about the needs of your brand and any sub-brands or associated brands that may become part of its future. An elevated brand is one that doesn't shy away from future thinking and is conscious of how it may need to change or adapt (or even just solidify where it currently stands with deeper roots) in years to come.

This may be through looking at the brand's future from these perspectives:

1. **Environment:** As your brand potentially grows or changes in the future, what impact might this have on your environment? Which systems are you instilling now to counteract any negative impact and how might you improve things for the future? This may be as simple as reducing your waste, partnering with an environmental cause, utilising land travel options vs flying wherever possible and/or looking at the ways you can remove inefficiencies. Or it may be as detailed as engaging an environmental consultant or hiring a permanent staff member to keep on top of this and challenge your practices now and into the future.

2. **Finance:** It is hard to move at pace or adapt to changing environments when you're worried about every single dollar. This is where the money mapping and business model work you did back in Chapter 5 is imperative. Unfortunately, many brands have gone under due to a mismanagement of financial resources and a blame game between people 'at the top'. A future-thinking brand is one that is able to monitor its financial standing at any point and makes considered investments in people, product and promotions.

3. **People:** How can you retain your top staff and how are you utilising succession planning to ensure these people stay engaged and working within the brand? How are you hiring not only for what the brand needs today, but also for what it may need in the future? How are you considering all of the people that may wish to engage or even be employed with your brand? How are you staying on top of labour needs and effective hiring policies? How do you facilitate a culture that truly nourishes its staff and encourages them to grow with the brand? In this category you also want to consider the social impact of your brand when it comes to your customers, suppliers, manufacturers and stockists. How is their data managed? How are you ensuring you are adhering to international labour standards and human rights across your entire supply chain?

4. **Product:** How adaptable is your product (be it a physical product or a service offering, or a mix of both) and does it need to be? For example, the funeral industry has roughly been the same for thousands of years across various religions, cultures and ethnicities. People will continue to die and the product offering doesn't necessarily need to change massively. On the other hand, the education industry is constantly changing and it needs to be aware of how people will choose to learn in the future, what they need to learn (particularly in certain sectors) and how lifestyle changes (such as more people working remotely or shifts in global migration) will impact this.

5. **Technology:** You don't have to jump on every new tech trend to be future thinking, but you must embrace and acknowledge the impact that technology has and will continue to have on your industry. How might your brand harness the power of emerging technologies to improve your services and products, in a way that still remains true to your purpose?

In Chapter 3 you conducted a SWOT analysis of your brand. Now, consider one of the five areas above (environment, finance, people, product and technology) and conduct a future-thinking SWOT analysis focusing on it.

For example, when it comes to the way you're thinking about the environment and your brand in the future, what are you doing well (Strengths)? What are you completely ignoring (Threats)? What could you be doing more of (Opportunities)? And where are you completely failing to consider your future impact (Weaknesses)?

Another framework that can help with future thinking is the Ansoff matrix (which we will dive into in Chapter 9).

Business *to* Brand

Elevation: Analytics and impact

More than a decade ago I headed up the Home and Kitchen team at Amazon UK – at the time the third biggest growth category for the brand. I often used to joke that you couldn't say hello at Amazon without backing it up with data and while that was a bit of a stretch, we did use data to make just about every decision. In the years since, and having now worked with thousands of other businesses – large and small – I believe it takes a mix of gut and data to understand what your brand is doing well and where it might improve.

An elevated brand is one that understands how to seek out data and, most importantly, how to utilise it to make educated decisions about its future. It is also one that accepts that there may be gaps between what it has promised its audience (e.g. we will deliver XYZ experience and we have these values underpinning our brand) and how its audience will perceive the truth of that promise.

One of the simplest ways to begin this process is to create a brand scorecard.

As the name suggests, a brand scorecard is a list of the things you want to measure your performance as a brand against. Much like a student's report card, a brand scorecard relays where you're excelling as well as where you may be falling short or need more focus.

(Like most things brand strategists can bring into a company, this can be an exciting project to be a part of, but I need to point out that it is only beneficial if it's actually maintained!)

To create your brand scorecard:

1. Take the time to consider what you most want to measure to ensure your brand is staying true to its promise. This may be how well it delivers on its purpose, goals, vision, people, values and connection objectives as well as things like brand loyalty, internal culture, brand positioning and more.

2. Decide on a platform or tool for recording the scores. This can be as basic as an Excel or Google Sheet, or as complicated as an online program designed to digitise all of this. If you have never done this before (and this might be a valid assumption given you're reading this book) I would opt for an easier solution so you can actually make a start vs procrastinating due to the program options available. One of my clients simply uses a whiteboard in their venue to capture this. Don't get stuck on finding the 'perfect' platform, just start somewhere.

3. Decide on the data you'll need to track and when (and by whom) it will be updated. For example, some data collection channels will have clear reports and numerical data you can pull from (e.g. GA4, your website/eCommerce platform or your revenue tracker/accounting or HR software), while other data channels may be more gut feel or anecdotal (say, stories from a focus group).

4. Input the list into your chosen platform or tool. Then, input a metric for each item. For example, under brand loyalty you may gather online reviews or data from your customer service team/tool to see how well/poorly you are performing. You may also have your social media manager or marketing person look at the types of comments and amplification happening for your brand that relate back to your brand values. With internal culture you may be looking at things like staff retention, whereas under revenue you may be looking at budgets or targets per week or the average transaction value (ATV) and even lifetime value (LV).

5. Look at the gaps and where you are underperforming. What is this down to? Resources? Skills? Misalignment? Systems?

6. Don't focus 100% on the negative. Also look at the areas that you're performing well in to see how some of your processes or brand actions are contributing to this. Could they be replicated across those gaps or areas you identified in Q5?

7. Put in place an action list between now and the next review.

Business *to* Brand

Elevation: Alignment

The final part of the ACE brand model is one of the most important and it is present throughout everything you do in your brand.

How aligned – authentically – is your brand to its mission and vision? How are your values and beliefs showing up in everything the brand does, internally and externally?

When we think of an incredible, authentic and elevated brand experience so much of what we are thinking about is not the logo or colour choice, it's the way the people, products and entire process makes us feel. It's about the total alignment between brand promise and brand delivery and the exceeding of expectations that makes us want to champion this brand.

So often business owners can start out super clear about their mission, vision and values, but somehow lose sight of these as the business and brand grows. Much like a soon-to-be parent who insists they will 'never do what my parents did' or 'I'll always put the child first' only to have life and circumstances get in the way of what they had originally promised.

So, how well are you doing? And what might you need to work on to truly be in alignment with what you set out to create with your brand? Where are you falling short? Is it a matter of skills? Systems? Staffing?

Consider a scenario in which you are completely aligned with the brand promise and where every single customer and client thinks, 'Yes, they did what they said they would' – how far/close are you to achieving this right now?

No brand, nor business for that matter, is perfect. But it's by choosing alignment at every stage that we can aim to be the best we possibly can be. How aligned is your brand right now? What would close that gap?

TASKS TO CONSIDER

Elevation of a brand is not an easy task and it's one that needs to be constantly assessed, interrogated and challenged in order to be successful.

Work through the following tasks or download them in a worksheet form online via the QR code below.

1. *Using the knowledge you have gained so far, work through the tasks for each of the elevation elements:*

    *   *connection channels*
    *   *people*
    *   *authority building*
    *   *future thinking*
    *   *analytics and impact*
    *   *alignment.*

2. *Revisit your answers in Figure 3.5 (page 62) and look at how you originally ranked these six elements for your brand.*

3. *Now that you have done the work (or come back to this when you have), where would you rank yourself now?*

4. *How has this changed? What further changes are necessary?*

5. *When will you take action on these? Get out the calendar and schedule this in.*

In the next chapter we dive into an important element of a brand to get right in order to elicit and retain trust.

Ready? Let's talk about consistency.

Scan for digital worksheet

08.

Why consistency is key

In 1859 Charles Dickens began his now-famous book *A Tale of Two Cities*, with the following paragraph: 'It was the best of times, it was the worst of times, it was the age of wisdom, it was the age of foolishness, it was the epoch of belief, it was the epoch of incredulity, it was the season of Light, it was the season of Darkness, it was the spring of hope, it was the winter of despair ...'

Now, Dickens may well have penned those words more than 150 years ago, but somehow they seem to epitomise what has been happening recently with various brands. Where some brands seem to understand how to bring their mission to life and stay in true alignment with their values and beliefs, others appear to think of their brand as little more than a cash machine wrapped up in great packaging.

Let me try to illustrate this with a tale of two brands and the differences between them.

In 2022, my husband and I decided to invest in a shelving unit from Vitsœ, after almost two decades of having one of their items on our wish list. Until then we hadn't had the permanent home, nor the money, to invest in a piece like this – which we knew would last a lifetime.

In the same year, my husband, an avid surfer and daily skater, began connecting with a surf brand based in the US. My husband, in his forties, isn't a huge fan of social media and is definitely not the type of guy to reach out to a brand and forge connections. But with this company he felt safe to do so. The brand was all about purpose and passion, and utilised the act of surfing – for men in their forties and fifties – as a vehicle for connection. When it announced a retreat, specifically for men who wanted to connect and share knowledge while also indulging in their love of surfing, my husband was in.

In both cases there was a little uncertainty. Neither company was based in Australia and both offers – the Vitsœ shelving unit and the US-based surf retreat – came at a considerable cost. We couldn't just go into a showroom and check the quality of the Vitsœ shelving in person and we didn't know anyone near us who owned one. Nor could my husband reach out to anyone who had been on the surf retreat as it was a new offering by the company.

In both cases we needed to take a little leap of faith that the brand's promise would be delivered.

So, what happened?

The Vitsœ relationship started with an initial email I sent, sharing our love for the company and what we hoped to achieve with the shelving. What came back was so much more than simply a welcome email sequence or a few lines with a PDF attached. Instead, it was a heartfelt thank you from one particular Vitsœ employee, who then discussed the options available and basically treated me as if I was his personal interior design client, asking me specific questions about the way we lived, what we would be storing in and on the shelves, where it would be positioned in the house and what we might want to consider before purchasing. There was no obligation, he said, to go forward but either way he was happy to help me figure out if this shelving unit was right for us. Numerous emails followed as he and I together figured out what would work given our walls were, at the time, made of logs and not flat like most.

Once we had decided on the type of shelving we would be buying, the same employee helped us through every single stage, from the ordering through to the shipping, through to tips on how to set it all up and even celebrated how it looked when I sent him a photo of it on our log cabin wall. In addition to this, the way in which the shelving was packed was so considered – not only for ease of construction and handling, but also for packing the unit up again if we decided to move. The seemingly tiny but incredibly useful details – such as customised spirit levels that clicked into place on the shelves, and even the little icon pointing upward on the railings so you knew which way they went – made the entire experience of putting together a shelving unit *enjoyable*, which is not a word most couples who have ever attempted to construct flat-packed items together would ever choose.

In short, the brand promise was absolutely delivered and the experience far exceeded anything we could have imagined. What's more, it instantly diluted any feelings we may have had about the cost of the product. The value from the consistent service was immeasurable.

If only the surf retreat company had considered, even for a moment, humanising and making consistent its customer journey.

After months of consideration and reviewing the marketing channels and content, my husband decided to send a direct message to the company on one of its social channels. He was not only keen to go to the surf retreat himself, but had also spoken with some surf-loving friends here in Australia and was considering how a few of them could get over there. First, he needed to know a rough idea of cost as this was a considerable factor in signing on. As I said, he is not a huge fan of social media and rarely, if ever, has contacted a brand through it. In this case, and having followed them closely, he felt okay to do so. He wrote to them about his connection with the brand, its vision and how much he wanted to support that by flying over from Australia to the US retreat. Could they please let him know how much it would be?

What he received was a simple '3800'. Not even a dollar sign or a 'Thank you so much for your support. The cost is $xxx', or even 'You can check out all the details over at website.com'. A can't-be-bothered response that not only cost the brand the business of my husband and his friends, but also instilled in my husband an instant distrust. As he said afterwards, 'All the stuff they purport to live by – deep connections, human relationships, quality conversations and slowing down to take the time for what's most important – none of that was present when I'd gone out of my way to connect with them.'

In the book *Positioning: The Battle for Your Mind*, Ries and Trout suggest that positioning goes hand in hand with consistency; that you have to show up day after day to cement that positioning. And as you now know, as a human species we crave consistency in order to create trusting, psychologically safe relationships. The same is true for brands. What can take years to build up and create in the minds of your audience can be undone in seconds when you fail to set up systems to celebrate and champion consistency in vision, values, visuals and voice.

So, how do you do this, especially when you may be working as a solo operator or within a small team?

In my experience working at massive global brands, as well as helping smaller brands get up and running in a way that's sustainably successful, I've found three things that are most helpful in promoting consistency:

1. setting up quality brand guidelines

2. creating supportive systems

3. monitoring feedback and being open to change.

Brand guidelines

Whether you call it your brand guide, brand DNA, brand strategy, brand bible or any other term, what you want to create is something that is accessible and easily understood by everyone in the company, and which relays the most important elements of your brand.

This will include much of what you have already worked on:

- purpose
- vision
- mission
- values and beliefs
- brand promise
- creations
- audience
- positioning and competition
- origins and naming story
- core brand messages
- tone of voice
- visual identity
- impact
- alignment.

It doesn't need to be a gigantic document – or even a document at all. You want this to be a living, breathing part of your brand, one that is easily understood and accessible to everyone working within the company. As such, it may be a series of videos like a mini Netflix for your brand where people can sign into an online portal, watch and engage with the various brand elements. Or it may be in the form of a book, landing page or even audio and visual podcast series.

Get creative in how you relay this information but make sure it *is* relayed.

In the early days of my business I would regularly consult on brand and marketing strategy to larger, usually corporate, clients. So often I would ask people working there what the overall vision was for the company, what they believed the business model to be and even where the brand name came from. Occasionally I would get someone who loved what they did and knew the answers, but a lot of the time I would be met with a shrug or a slightly embarrassed 'not really sure' response.

For a brand to be consistent, its staff must be aware of what it's trying to do, why it was started and how it views its future vision – not just in the onboarding phase but consistently throughout their time working there. While you may not wish to share every single financial detail, the key elements of your brand must be shared, understood and then sent out into the world to ensure everyone encountering the brand has a consistent and quality experience.

Don't get fooled into thinking that once the brand guidelines are done, it is complete, never to be edited again. This document is a living part of your brand and one that must be reviewed, analysed, updated and shared frequently. This may mean bringing up elements within weekly business review meetings; designing and making visible your mission, vision and values in your physical locations; measuring campaigns and activity against your vision, mission and values; and checking in regularly with your audiences. It may also mean showing where the brand is positioned on a quarterly basis and analysing if it's moving towards/further away from its goal.

Likewise, part of this information may well be shown on your website, in your physical locations (if you have them), email signatures and email sequences. Much like the brand scorecard, your brand guidelines should help when it comes to staff reviews, campaign and business-as-usual marketing, as well as the hiring process.

Setting up your systems

In the work I have done with smaller company owners in my own business and in the years before that, I have found seven clear steps to setting up systems that work for your business.

Dr W Edwards Deming, an engineer, statistician, professor, author and well-known management consultant, suggested in his book *Out of the Crisis* that up to 94% of challenges and ideas for improvement result from a lack of systems, rather than directly as a result of people not caring about their role.

Be really honest with yourself and consider how well your systems support the brand vision. Are your staff genuinely set up for success?

Here are my seven steps to great systems:

1. Identify business functions
2. Understand the outputs of each function
3. Map out the processes (for those that work and those that don't work)
4. Identify the leaks
5. Test, test and test again
6. Set an implementation deadline
7. Review and improve.

Let's break these down in a bit more detail so you can set these up for your brand.

Identify business functions

The first thing to consider is what your brand actually does. What are the different functions of it? For example, with My Daily Business, we have the following business functions:

- Marketing
- HR/People management
- Sales
- Production
- Finance
- Design.

From this, consider which functions are absolutely essential to the brand itself. You may also want to add in any functions that you haven't considered but are necessary, especially as you grow. For example, as someone working on their own you may think HR is not needed; however, you may well need things like professional development, training, insurance policies and contracts.

Consider:

- What is it that your business does?
- Which functions are essential?
- Which functions might you have forgotten or dismissed altogether?

Once you have your functions, list them out using an Excel or Google Sheet with each function being the first cell in a column.

Understand the outputs of each function

The second step is to list out the outputs or deliveries for each of these functions. For example under 'Marketing' you may have:

- social media
- press releases
- video
- podcast
- opt-ins/lead generation
- email marketing
- print collateral
- visual merchandising.

Under HR you may have:

- weekly 1:1s
- quarterly reviews
- monthly team bonding
- quarterly offsite
- insurances and policies
- professional development (PD) training.

Map out the processes

The next step is to figure out the outputs that already have a great process and are in alignment with your brand's mission and the outputs that need focus.

For the processes that ARE working well, consider:

- Is there a checklist or documentation for these processes (even in your head)?
- If not, can you create one? Remember, process documentation can be a great way to showcase your brand values. If one of your values is 'fun', how can you make this whole thing more fun? If one is 'creative', how can this become a creative process? Utilising mediums like video and audio can be more engaging vs a plain-text document.
- Has one person been doing this process for a while and so may have their own way of doing things? Is it documented?
- Ask why these processes are working well and document the reasons.
- Get buy-in from anyone who is involved in this process.

For example with My Daily Business, our podcast process under the function of marketing works well. We would then work through the steps above to look at why it's working well. This might include things such as clear process documentation, four people working on each episode and each knowing exactly what they are responsible for and when to move their part onto the next person, forward planning of what is coming up and when, scheduled weekly times for recording, editing and transcribing, email and graphic templates for promotion. And so on.

All of this is documented in our internal project management system and we review this quarterly and make any necessary changes. From a brand perspective, we use our key brand messages and content pillars to come up with and plan out six to twelve months of content at any one time. We also ensure that we are living up to the brand values with our selection of guests, topics, advertisers and partners, freebies and other materials associated with the podcast.

Next, for the processes that ARE NOT working well, write down the ideal scenario for the process from start to finish in a series of steps (draw a straight line/arrow like the one below in Figure 8.1).

Figure 8.1 **Ideal scenario process planning**

First step   **Ideal result**

In doing this you may realise other documents will need to be created. For example, the eCommerce example in Figure 8.2 on the opposite page shows the need for online shoot templates to be created, so that imagery will be consistent and on brand.

Why consistency is key

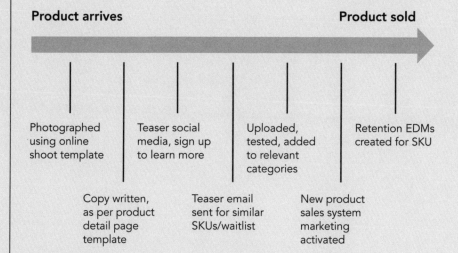

Figure 8.2 **Example process map for adding inventory to eCommerce site**

After mapping out the ideal scenario you want to:

- identify why these steps don't currently exist (e.g. is it an issue with resources? Skills? Time? Customer demand?)

- identify the long-term cost of not developing these processes (this is not just about financial costs – what impact will this have on your brand's reputation and trust between brand and audience?)

- figure out a timeline to create and document these processes

- create and document processes in a software system that everyone can access and which can easily be updated.

Business *to* Brand

Identify the leaks

Benjamin Franklin once proclaimed that 'a small leak will sink a great ship'.

Think back to the story I shared at the start of this chapter about the US surf retreat. That small leak – the inability for someone to consider their response to a heartfelt Instagram DM – not only led to a missed sales opportunity but also to an entire shift from a brand being admired to being discarded.

Once you have created and documented your processes you want to:

- check for clarity – can they be easily understood?
- ensure the file naming is clear and that everyone involved knows where they are housed. (e.g. are you using Dropbox? Google Drive? Slack? Asana? Notion?)
- check that you're not making assumptions about anything. Don't assume he/she/they know it. They don't.
- add any steps into your process to make it crystal clear what is expected.

Test, test and test again

Assumptions kill systems. When a system is set up well, there should be no room for assumptions to ruin it. This is where testing comes in. You want to test, test and test again that the process can be understood and easily followed.

How?

Ask someone who has nothing to do with the process (either another staff member or a friend) to review it.

- Can they complete the task/steps required based on the process you have created and documented (skills aside)?
- Do they understand how to follow the steps?

If not, review and revise the steps, then test again.

Set an implementation deadline

It's one thing to create a new process, it's quite another to actually implement it. Set a deadline for when this process will be in full swing.

For example, you may give people (or yourself if you're a solo operator) two to three weeks to get it down, test it again or add to it. From then on, this process should be 'the way'.

(That is, of course, until the final step.)

Review and improve

Like anything else in business, processes should never be 'set and forget'. Set up a series of future reviews for the processes within each business function. Look at what's working and what could be improved.

You may decide on a frequency for the reviews, such as quarterly, and add them into your schedule now. Add a feedback loop a fortnight prior to each review to capture feedback ahead of time, use the review efficiently and act accordingly.

Another huge part of a consistent brand is understanding what's coming up for you and ensuring you stay consistent with your message and the way the brand is presented – having a system or process in place can assist with this.

One useful tool is a basic At-A-Glance calendar. I am always pleasantly surprised at what a gigantic impact this simple framework can have, even at larger brands that have numerous people within their marketing and communications teams. And it's not only great for marketing but for all parts of your business.

So, how do you create it?

It's as simple as drawing up twelve boxes, much like the example in Figure 8.3 (page 204).

Figure 8.3 **Your At-A-Glance calendar (aka)**

Your Awesome Year (YAY) Calendar

JANUARY	FEBRUARY	MARCH

APRIL	MAY	JUNE

JULY	AUGUST	SEPTEMBER

OCTOBER	NOVEMBER	DECEMBER

Once you have it drawn up, input important information such as:

- key brand campaigns
- key dates that impact your brand or audience including those for your industry and location (e.g. Design dates in the UK) and causes you wish to support (e.g. World Mental Health Day)
- key collection or new product rollout dates
- dates you/your staff will be on holidays
- dates for causes that tie in with your brand.

From here you can begin to plan your brand communications and brand activity around these dates and key periods, particularly if key people are going to be away or if your brand is aligned with certain causes.

A great example of this happened while writing this book, when I emailed the team at Tony's Chocolonely about their interview. I was sent an automated message that read: 'It's the UN International Day for the Remembrance of the Slave Trade and its Abolition. Team Tony's UK are taking the day out to educate ourselves and reflect on how our colonial past has shaped us.'

This is a fantastic example of a brand walking the talk and showing up consistently, not only on social media or larger platforms that are customer-facing but also within the brand's internal culture. Life is hectic at times and having a plan can enable you to show up as consistently as possible, without missing dates that are important to your brand's mission and vision.

One last note about systems. As discussed in Chapter 7, people are a huge part of a brand's success. What systems do you have set up to measure their engagement with their work? What will you be doing to ensure they also love what they do on the daily?

Now, let's move on. The last way to stay consistent in a business can only really come into fruition and have a real impact on your brand consistency if the first two – brand guidelines and supportive systems – are adopted.

Monitoring feedback and being open to change

One of the best TV shows, I believe, to have come out in recent years is *Couples Therapy* (both the US and Australian versions). In this show (yet another reality TV show #OwningIt) couples meet with a psychologist and share their challenges, fears, heartbreaks and celebrations. The couples that get the most out of the therapy experience are those who are open to truly listening, asking for feedback and acting on it to change.

In the same way, brands that remain consistent are those that listen and request feedback – and not only are they open to receiving feedback, but also to changing when required. In late 2022 the brand Anya Hindmarch launched Anya Hindmarch Rental, a capsule collection of top bags and accessory styles (new and archive) that people could rent by the day. This not only aligns with the brand's vision of creating conscious and long-term sustainability in the fashion industry, but also likely acts as a response to feedback from customers who may not necessarily want to buy products they may only use a few times.

Likewise, ten years earlier, the founders of Warby Parker gathered brand feedback prior to opening bricks-and-mortar stores. Using a refurbished school bus that internally replicated the inside of an eyewear store, the brand covered sixteen US cities in fifteen months, meeting fans, having them use the 'store' and gaining feedback as to what people in various cities most wanted from an eyewear store. This conscious effort to garner feedback resulted in a deeper understanding of how the brand could launch physical stores, as well as the elements of service in those stores that would need to be consistent and strong to encourage brand loyalty.

How are you eliciting feedback from your audience/s? What processes do you have in place to capture this feedback, analyse it and use it to fuel future actions?

Ways in which you can gather feedback for your brand include:

- post-purchase polls
- social listening (via your own staff or social listening software)
- customer/client satisfaction surveys
- phone calls
- email requests.

Decide on the tools you want to use, set a frequency for collecting this information and ensure that it's part of your processes from here on in. For example, after every coaching client finishes a package with us, they receive a detailed questionnaire about their experience. We then review these quarterly to see where we might improve things to ensure genuine and authentic alignment with our brand purpose and promise.

TASKS TO CONSIDER

Staying consistent in your brand takes work and isn't something you'll rectify overnight. But by working through the steps outlined in this chapter you'll be a lot closer to achieving it. Remember this is not a 'set and forget' element of business, but rather one that must be reviewed, well, consistently!

Utilising the knowledge you have gained so far, work through the following questions or download these in a worksheet form online via the QR code below.

1. *Do you have brand guidelines? If so, when was the last time you updated and shared them? If not, why? When can you start putting these guidelines together?*

2. *How might you amend or create brand guidelines that tie into your brand personality and tone of voice? Could you use another platform or medium (such as video) to create these going forward?*

3. *Considering the buyer cycle for your brand, where are people most likely to fall off? Where might your systems be lacking? You can revisit what the buyer cycle looks like on page 37.*

4. *Work through the seven steps to creating better systems. (If you want to dive deeper into this, check out our systems course at mydailybusiness.com/courses)*

5. *When can you begin to plan out your At-A-Glance calendar? Which dates will you need to include? Who else will need to be involved?*

6. *How might your brand walk the talk and show up to causes it champions in the same way that Tony's Chocolonely has?*

7. *Work through the list of feedback sources (e.g. post-purchase polls, satisfaction surveys) and decide on which you will use, if you're not already. Then consider how you can make them part of your processes going forwards and when you will review and action any insights.*

Once you have your brand guidelines, systems and feedback ideas in place, it's time to talk about the future of your brand. Let's go.

Scan for digital worksheet

Business *to* Brand

09.

Considering the future

In 2018 my husband and I decided to spend a few weeks travelling the North Island of New Zealand. It was the last year we had our (then only) son at home before he would start primary school and we figured this was a fantastic opportunity to visit friends and to see some of what is often considered to be one of the most beautiful countries on earth.

I apologise to any New Zealand readers for what I'm about to admit, but as someone who had grown up in Australia, I imagined that New Zealand – purely because of its geographical proximity – would offer a very similar visual experience to that of travelling across my own country. I imagined the scenery would be much the same, the wildlife and bush mirroring what I had grown up with (but with more kiwis than koalas). I was interested to learn more about the Māori culture and history, but other than that and seeing a very close friend I hadn't seen in years, I was unconvinced that New Zealand would offer that much difference.

I couldn't have been more wrong. The differences between Australia and New Zealand were vast – epic deep forests, which reminded me of travelling through Germany, would give way to tropical landscapes almost reminiscent of Fiji, before tremendous mountain views would take their place. The sights alone were beyond anything I could have imagined and as we worked our way around the North Island, I was constantly taken aback by its beauty.

On one of our final nights in New Zealand, we found ourselves exploring a campground just as the sun was beginning to set. As my husband dealt with some issues in our mini campervan, my then four-year-old son and I walked around the grounds, stopping every now and then to take in a native bird or a picturesque waterfall. As we wandered back to the campsite and along the toilet block, my son suddenly stopped and asked in bewilderment, 'Mama, what's that?'

I had to laugh because before us stood a public telephone box, complete with 1990s telco branding. As I explained to my son what used to happen before mobile phones came along, it dawned on me just how much has changed in the space of a generation. Since then we have had numerous conversations about 'the olden days' (aka the 1990s) and often I find myself explaining past experiences I genuinely loved that no longer exist: borrowing videos at Blockbuster, browsing new magazines at Borders and waiting for my roll of Kodak film to be developed at a chemist.

It's a fact of life that with age comes change. That said, I can't help but wonder if certain brands might still be around if they had invested a little more time in considering their future.

Five considerations for the future

So, how do you do this? You might think it's simply a case of looking at emerging technologies and somehow incorporating them into your brand – but there's a little more to it.

While none of us can predict the future, I've found in my work that there are strategies that can be implemented to have a better understanding of what is coming and the impact it may have on your brand.

These are divided into five key categories.

1. Environment

2. Finance

3. Product

4. People

5. Technology.

Environment

There is no denying the negative impact that humans are having on the planet. Everyone has their role to play, but businesses that are making money by selling products and services often have a direct environmental impact.

People are, quite rightly, expecting more from the brands they connect with (whether as an employee, supplier, stockist, customer or someone who likes your content on social media) and having an environmental policy is no longer a choice, but a requirement. So how will your brand reduce its impact on the environment in years to come? What can you start doing now – no matter how small – that can, with compound effort, have a positive impact on the environment in the future?

For product-based businesses this may be reviewing the packaging and production processes for the business as well as the afterlife of the product itself. What happens when people don't wish to use it anymore? Can it have another use? Is it truly designed to last? Can it be recycled via your channels? Can it be reconfigured in some way? Can you go deeper and improve current product lines rather than coming up with new new new? For service-based businesses it may be looking at your circular waste management system as well as things like digital filing. According to Greenly, data storage currently makes up 2% of global carbon emissions and accounts for more carbon emissions than the commercial airline industry.

How often are you, as a brand, reviewing your impact on the environment and how can you make this part of your normal routine? How often are you looking at other, less impactful, ways of doing business – from your travel (trains vs planes) through to the food you stock in your kitchen (from local farms vs brought in from the other side of the globe)?

How often are you auditing your business and overall brand through an environmental lens?

Finance

Cash flow, or the lack of, is one of the most common reasons for businesses to close down. You can have an incredibly purpose-led brand, but without a positive cash flow and an intimate awareness of your finances, it won't be around long enough to actually make an impact.

Future thinking when it comes to your finances is crucial to long-term success. Too often business owners will only look at their finances with any sort of scrutiny when there's nothing they can actively do to change the result (e.g. a retrospective review at tax time or a review when payments bounce or a significant purchase must be made). Future thinking is all about ensuring you have adequate financial systems in place to balance the financial needs of the business as it stands today with what it will look like tomorrow.

For example, when considering the overarching vision for the brand, who else will you need to employ in the next three to five years? Will your premises need to be changed or updated? Will your equipment need an overhaul? Which tech platforms and tools might you need to invest in? Where is the capital for this coming from?

How will you fund your future?

Another element to consider when you're looking at the future, financially, for your brand are things like inflation and global economic changes that may pose a risk for some of your products selection, your pricing strategy, and even you're hiring and retention of staff. How are you staying up to date with these elements and how are you future-proofing the above to ward off potential stress and financial pressure in the years to come?

Product

Your product includes your service offerings, physical products or any mix of these you offer including experiences. What you want to consider is how much your product offerings have changed since you began the brand and what changes you believe people will want, if any, in the future. Will people still need what your brand offers and how might this change in the future? It can be easy here to think that you simply don't need to change at all.

Let's take the funeral industry as an example.

While many people will be happy to go with the status quo and use the 'products' that have been around for thousands of years for their particular cultural and religious beliefs, the brand experience will be what sets you apart from competitors. Coming out of the COVID-19 pandemic, people may now expect a funeral to be live-streamed for family and friends who cannot make it in person. They may also expect digital versions of an order of service, a Spotify playlist of songs used in the service and/or a way of donating to a cause rather than sending flowers. So how can a funeral brand create an even better product? It may choose to look at the environmental impact of the death industry and offer some sort of carbon offset or tree planting as part of its packages. It may go one step further and work with a grief psychology practice to offer one-off or ongoing family grief counselling, or even meditation or breathwork activities for use within the first twelve months after a death. It may take the photos used in the service and create a book, a tangible memory of the person's life, or it may help the family in setting up an anniversary event twelve months after the death.

When you consider the products or services that your brand offers, what would make for an even better brand experience? What are people hoping for today that they will just expect tomorrow? What does their total life cycle look like?

How might a tweak in your product or service take you from running a good business to a great brand?

People

In Chapter 7 we looked at the crucial role that people within your brand play in your overall success. When it comes to future thinking, consider what your current and potential employees will expect from the brand in years to come.

In 2022 Australian Prime Minister Anthony Albanese passed a law that requires employers to grant ten days of paid leave to anyone who needs to flee a family and domestic violence situation, which was enacted in 2023. In the same year the Workplace Gender Equality Amendment (Closing the Gender Pay Gap) Bill 2023 was passed in parliament, which has led to companies with 100 or more staff having to report gender pay disparities, which will then be published publicly.

Elements like this are, rightly, becoming expected by staff. So how will you talk to their needs (present and future) with your own internal policies, procedures and processes? What are your policies around harassment, corruption/bribery and bullying?

Likewise, what are you doing to ensure you're hiring people who are not only committed to the brand but who can also grow with the brand in the future? When and how often are you reviewing your staff and succession planning? How often are you providing feedback to your staff so they feel valued and seen? What is your policy around training and upskilling staff? Does professional development exist and how will you financially forecast it and manage it from a time perspective?

Future thinking about people also extends to your suppliers. How will you continue to work with them and nurture great relationships, and ensure they are adhering to human rights and labour standards and creating ethically and psychologically safe environments for their staff? How often are you able to connect IRL?

When considering the future of people and your brand, you also want to consider global shifts that may mean a change in the way you manufacture and operate your business, as well as the causes you support and brands you collaborate with. A fantastic book that looks at the changing face of global innovation and the issues with the way many businesses in the West operate and what this means for business is *The Heart of A Cheetah: How We Have Been Lied to about African Poverty, and What That Means for Human Flourishing* by Magatte Wade. As the world becomes more global and all people understand the damage done to many countries and their populations by businesses (particularly in the West) the more all brands need to take responsibility and understand their way forward.

It is also about your customers and clients. What are you putting in place, or what will you need to put in place, to ensure their data remains protected? What will you be doing in the future to ensure everyone feels welcome and safe within your organisation, stores and physical locations?

Technology

I am from the last generation that grew up without the internet. It launched in Australia at the end of my final year at high school and for the first few years I was at university, few people used it for anything more than a Hotmail account they would check every few days. In the space of twenty years we have embraced changes in technology that we couldn't have ever predicted.

As a sociology major, I was required to read a lot of Dostoevsky, and there is one quote at the start of *The House of the Dead* that I think sums up our relationship with technology: 'Man is a creature that can get accustomed to anything, and I think that is the best definition of him.'

For a brand to be future thinking, there has to be some level of acceptance – and even embracing – of technology and all its advancements.

So, how will you embrace what technology can offer?

The answer lies in understanding your audience and brand vision, and what the two will need in the future.

How might you use technology to better understand, and even predict, what your customers and clients will want more of in the future? Is there a gap in your customer journey that tech can close? How might your use of tools like AI and automation allow you to become a more efficient business and enable your staff to have more time back to really consider how to drive the brand's vision forward?

Social media, for all its issues, has transformed the way small business owners can get in front of their audience without having to invest massively in traditional marketing. In one platform they gain access to focus groups, beta testers, magnetic content ideas and analytics.

Enable yourself to utilise the tech and not for the tech to utilise you.

Ansoff matrix

One last tool that can help when considering the future of your brand is the Ansoff matrix (see Figure 9.1 below).

Created by H Igor Ansoff, a Russian mathematician and business analyst, and first published in a 1957 article he penned for the *Harvard Business Review*, the Ansoff matrix is all about understanding how to strategically grow a business.

Figure 9.1 **The Ansoff matrix**

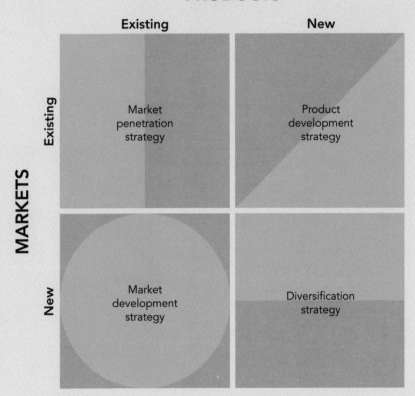

Business *to* Brand

On the Y-axis (vertical) you have new and existing markets, while on the X-axis (horizontal) you have new and existing products. From here you end up with four main areas for potential growth:

1. Market penetration: existing products in existing markets

2. Market development: existing products in new markets

3. Product development: new products for existing markets

4. Diversification: new products for new markets.

When considering the future of your brand, which of the four quadrants most applies to you?

For some brands, future growth may simply focus on gaining market penetration and positioning your business as the go-to brand for XYZ utilising existing products in the existing market you're in. For others, future growth for the brand may look like taking your existing products into new territories or to new audiences.

I may be going against the masses here, but I don't believe in growth purely for the sake of it. Brand growth must be in line with your overall vision and values to feel authentic.

What else should we know when it comes to future thinking? Why not ask a futurist?

Considering the future

Petah Marian

Futurist and trend forecaster

Petah Marian is an award-winning futurist and journalist with almost two decades' experience working across the retail and lifestyle sectors. At the forefront of shaping tomorrow's world, Petah's expertise lies in identifying emerging consumer and macro shifts, translating them into strategies that help organisations futureproof their propositions.

Image: Jodi Hinds (jodihinds.com)

What is a futurist?

A futurist is a person who does research to consider what the future will look like to help organisations understand what kinds of opportunities are likely to emerge in various scenarios.

What are the sorts of things a futurist looks at when it comes to business and brand?

We take a holistic view to look at all of the things that influence a person's life – from politics and economics through to technology, creativity, sociology and anthropology to create a picture of a brand or future brand's customers to figure out what they're likely to want from the products that they may buy. We look at everything from how people might want to shop, through to what colours will resonate.

What are some of the tactics you employ to understand what is happening now and what will happen in the future when it comes to things like trends, buying behaviour and social change?

There is a huge amount of research that takes place, often it's good to look at what's happening elsewhere in the world. China is quite far ahead of Western countries when it comes to online buying behaviours, so that's a great point of interest. But also it's good to look at things like economic forecasts to understand how inflation might change the kinds of brands and products that people will want to buy.

If you were to give advice to someone transforming their current small business into a brand that will be around for years to come, what would you say?

You don't need to follow every trend. Finding the balance between consistency and newness is important. The reason that brands become successful and have longevity is because they understand a set of consumer needs and consistently tap into them, without getting stagnant or boring.

Are there platforms or tools that can help people un-code the future for their own industry or sector?

There are a number of platforms – The Future Laboratory, Stylus, and WGSN are all subscription-based tools that people can use to understand emerging trends. Brands can also work with independent consultants that will help them create a unique proposition.

Business *to* Brand

When it comes to tech and the speed at which is it changing, how can people stay ahead of the curve? Should they even be trying to?

Only if that's where your customer is headed. Having a strong understanding of what your customer likes, how they spend their time and what kinds of devices or platforms they use (or are likely to use) is what should drive your strategy. For instance, it doesn't make sense to invest heavily in a metaverse/NFT strategy if your primary customer is a Boomer man who is not spending much time on social media, and is unlikely to realise any value from a digital collectable.

When we think about future forecasting so often people turn straight to tech and tech only. Are there traditional elements of business you feel will still matter in decades to come?

Technology is only an enabler. It's incredibly important to overlay the human experience on top of that to understand what kinds of technologies will impact your business or if it's even relevant to your target customer. One of the things that Amazon often looks at are the things that are unlikely to change, and confidently invests in them – for instance, they believe people will always want to feel like they get good value and fast delivery. Beyond these things, when I think about brand values that are likely to remain consistent, people will want to feel a sense of belonging and connection to brands that they identify with, and sustainability will continue to be increasingly important.

What do you think the biggest myth is surrounding building a brand today?

That you need to appeal to all people all the time. Having a strong and decently sized niche with a solid point of view is better than trying to appeal to everybody.

Web: petahmarian.com

TASKS TO CONSIDER

On a very practical level, it can feel daunting to consider the future for your brand. While it can be somewhat easier to consider your day-to-day activities, or even the exciting long-term vision, what can be harder is to consider the tasks you need to do today and systems that need to be set up to help your brand tomorrow.

Utilising the knowledge you have gained so far, work through the following questions or download these in a worksheet form online via the QR code below.

1. *When it comes to the future of your brand, where do you see it in the next ten years? How do you feel about this projection?*

2. *What scares you the most about the future of your brand?*

3. *Which of the categories discussed (environment, finance, people, product and technology) stands out as the most important for your brand? Why is this?*

4. *Schedule in time over the next twelve months to work on implementing the most important outcomes from your work in Q3. Ensure that you get input from everyone who needs to be involved.*

5. *Where might you invest more time in researching the future trends for your own brand? Which platforms or people will help you do this? (You can find a list of companies that specialise in this on our resources page at mydailybusiness.com/brandbook.)*

Before we jump into Chapter 10, where we look at the nitty-gritty daily actions you'll need to take, we will hear from Sandra Velasquez, the 'Nuestra Jefa' (boss) and founder of Latina beauty and skincare brand, Nopalera.

Scan for digital
worksheet

Image: Amanda López (amandalopezphoto.com)

Profile: *Nopalera*

Raised by Mexican immigrant parents in California, Sandra Velasquez grew up surrounded by determined, proud, resilient and resourceful family and friends. Inspired by this boldness she created a beauty and skincare brand that would remind those who engage with it of their own resilience, beauty, power and strength. Named Nopalera, after the nopal cactus, the brand continues to gain recognition for its quality ingredients, stunning designs and heartfelt ethos. Here's what founder Sandra Velasquez had to say about building a brand.

'We are building a Latina legacy brand – one that will outlive all of us. The real brands last for decades or even centuries. In one hundred years we will still be inspiring people to stand in their worth. It's a timeless message.'

What do you believe is the difference between running a business and being the custodian of a brand?

I intentionally set out to create a brand that was bold, colourful, and clearly Latina. I wanted the Latin@ community to feel proud and seen, when they saw Nopalera. The support has been incredible from the community. I am the protector of the brand that also happens to be a business.

Where did the name for the brand come from and can you describe how your upbringing has influenced the brand and its offerings?

Nopalera is the name of the cactus plant when it's still in the ground. Once you cut off the 'pencas' or pads to eat, they are referred to as nopales. They are one of the most resilient, regenerative and versatile crops in the world. We use them for food, body care and textiles like vegan leather. What other plant does that? Because it was abundant growing up I took it for granted. It was staring me in the face my whole life.

Your brand is so much more than simply its products. Its celebration of Mexican culture and people is so meaningful. Its message 'remain resilient' couldn't be more aligned with today's world. Was it scary to put so much of yourself into your brand or did it just come naturally?

Thankfully I was a professional musician before launching Nopalera so I had twenty years of experience putting myself out there. I still get nervous but I focus on the mission and impact and that gets me through. I would advise anyone looking to start a brand to focus on the customer. Your brand is not about you.

What have been some of the best brand activations or collaborations or campaigns you have taken part in and how do you choose which to do, especially when the brand has gained more media attention and, therefore, perhaps more offers over its time?

The best activation we have done are our own pop-ups at our boutiques. It's a win-win. We shine the light on our retail partners and engage with our community.

The beauty and skincare industry is gigantic but with that size also comes competition. How have you been able to stand out as a brand in such a massive industry and what advice would you give to others who perhaps think it's too hard?

A few key things: make sure your product solves a problem; know who your customer is and what they care about; invest in branding; and understand margins and know your numbers.

What do you think the biggest myth is around the idea of building a brand today?

That having a good product that works is enough. Lots of products are good. You still need a strong brand that has an emotional connection and is memorable.

How has your vision for the company changed over time, or has it remained the same now as it was at the beginning?

Our mission has been the same from the beginning: to create a bolder body experience powered by Mexico nopal cactus. We want to change the narrative about the value of Latino goods in the market and therefore our own value as a community. I hope to inspire others to take bold action and fully be themselves.

What legacy would you like Nopalera to leave behind?

The impact is to change culture. When you think of Latino goods you don't think 'value' or cheap. You think elevated and valuable.

What's the best business advice you have received that you wish you had known when you were starting your brand?

Create your CEO schedule and protect your time. You have to create boundaries for yourself otherwise you'll grind yourself to the ground and that will affect your company negatively. And if you find yourself drowning, that's when you know you need to hire some help, even just a few hours a week makes a world of difference.

Why do you think building a brand, and not simply a business, is important today?

We are building a Latina legacy brand – one that will outlive all of us. The real brands last for decades or even centuries. In one hundred years we will still be inspiring people to stand in their worth. It's a timeless message.

Web: nopalera.co

IG: @nopalera.co

TT: @nopalera.co

'I still get nervous but I focus on the mission and impact and that gets me through. I would advise anyone looking to start a brand to focus on the customer. Your brand is not about you.'

Image: Amanda López (amandalopezphoto.com)

Business *to* Brand

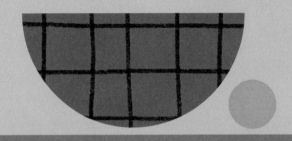

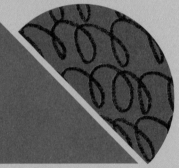
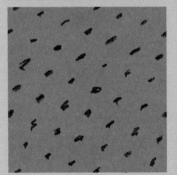

10.

What are you doing on the daily?

There are some moments in a friendship where, no matter what else is happening or how long it has been between catch-ups, you absolutely must show up. One of those is when a friend experiences the loss of a parent. As someone who lost both of my parents in my thirties, I will always remember the friends who attended my parents' funerals and those who found something else to do that day.

So when a close friend texted me a few years back to inform me that her beloved dad had died, I knew I wanted to attend the funeral regardless of what else was going on. As Dr Brené Brown wrote in *Braving the Wilderness: The Quest for True Belonging and the Courage to Stand Alone*: 'When I asked participants to identify three to five specific behaviours that their friends, family and colleagues do that raise their level of trust with them, funerals always emerged in the top three responses. Funerals matter. Showing up to them matters. And funerals matter not just to the people grieving, but to everyone who is there. The collective pain (and sometimes joy) we experience when gathering in any way to celebrate the end of a life is perhaps one of the most powerful experiences of inextricable connection.'

As I entered the funeral, I collected one of the orders of service booklets that showed photos of my friend's father, as well as the multi-generational family he had helped create. On my way home, while stuck in a rush-hour traffic jam, I looked through the booklet in more detail, in particular at the prose on the inside cover.

The words – written in 2003 by author Michael Josephson – made such an impact that, once home, I stuck it on the top of my fridge, right at eye level, so I could be reminded of them on a daily basis.

They read:

> Ready or not, someday it will all come to an end
> There will be no more sunrises, no minutes, hours or days
> All the things you collected, whether treasured or forgotten,
> Will pass to someone else.
>
> Your wealth, fame and temporal power will shrivel to irrelevance.
> It will not matter what you owned or what you were owed.
> The wins and losses that once seemed so important will fade away.
>
> It won't matter where you came from,
> Or on what side of the tracks you lived.
> At the end whether you were beautiful or brilliant,
> Male or female, even your skin colour won't matter.
>
> So what will matter? How will the value of your days be measured?
> What will matter is not what you bought, but what you built,
> Not what you got but what you gave.
>
> What will matter is not your success, but your significance.
> What will matter is not what you learned, but what you taught.
> What will matter is every act of integrity, compassion and courage
> Or sacrifice that enriched, empowered or encouraged others.

What are you doing on the daily?

What will matter is not your competence, but your character.
What will matter is not how many people you knew,
But how many will feel a lasting loss when you are gone.

What will matter is not your memories, but the memories
That live in those who loved you.

Living a life that matters doesn't happen by accident.
It's not a matter of circumstance but of choice.
You chose to live a life that mattered.

Copyright 2003, Michael Josephson (josephsoninstitute.org)

In all parts of our lives – from the businesses and brands we operate through to the personal relationships we build – we are required to show up and keep showing up. It's when we fail to keep showing up and doing the work, on the daily, that things begin to unravel and, if left in that state, potentially fall apart.

My dear dad did the newspaper crossword every single day. My late father-in-law ran through a routine of callisthenics, yoga and meditation before work each morning. Both men understood that small steps add up and that strength, mental and physical, works much like compound interest – what starts off small can accumulate at an exponential pace.

The same can be said for showing up in full alignment with your brand on the daily. While it may feel in the moment like a small action towards bringing your vision to life, consistent, genuine work adds up. As Josephson said, 'Living a life that matters doesn't happen by accident. It's not a matter of circumstance but of choice'.

Business *to* Brand

You choose it. In the same way you choose the daily actions you will take to create an ACE brand that's about more than the financials.

What makes a great brand experience and how do you ensure this happens, on the daily?

It starts with planning.

It would be nice to think that your brand vision and values are just so ingrained in your psyche that you don't need to forward plan or spend time considering how to show up in alignment but – like with so many things in life – it only becomes ingrained through practice and planning.

Remember in Chapter 4 when I shared my first 'driving' lesson with my father? That was more than twenty-five years ago. Since then, I've been in the driver's seat for at least 150,000 kilometres, the equivalent of driving to Amsterdam from Melbourne five times. It makes sense then that driving is something I can do almost on autopilot.

I want you (and your team) to get to a state where your brand vision, mission, values and beliefs, audience needs and business objectives are so clearly defined and reiterated so often that you're absolutely consistent in showing up to them, on the daily.

Until that point, you'll need to put planning and processes in place.

What are you doing on the daily?

Getting on the same page

In Chapter 8 we looked at why consistency matters and how you can ensure consistency through the use of brand guidelines, supportive systems and monitoring feedback. Internally, consider how you're bringing the brand guidelines to life, not just in the onboarding stage or at annual review time, but all year round.

Seth Godin sends an email, based on his blog, every single day. Sometimes they are multiple paragraphs in length, sometimes it's simply one sentence. By showing up daily, he is reiterating to the recipient's mind that he is an expert in his field, and also just a human connecting with another human (or thousands of them) via his thoughts in text format. (You can sign up yourself at seths.blog/subscribe.)

To create a genuinely ACE brand, you want everyone working in and around the brand to be able to clearly articulate how it is authentic, creative and elevated.

Here are some questions you'll want to ask yourself in relation to the brand you're building.

BRAND ELEMENT	QUESTIONS TO ASK
AREA: AUTHENTICITY	
Purpose Vision Mission Values and beliefs Creations Audiences	Do your employees/staff/suppliers know your overall brand vision? What about your brand values and beliefs? What is your process for measuring brand activity against your vision, mission and value? Where in each week are you asking 'How are we delivering on our brand promise?' and how can this become part of your weekly process?

BRAND ELEMENT	QUESTIONS TO ASK
AREA: CREATIVITY	

BRAND ELEMENT	QUESTIONS TO ASK
Positioning	How are you ensuring you keep your desired position in your audience's minds? What are you doing monthly, weekly and daily to maintain it?
Competition	How often are you reviewing your competition? What lessons are you learning from them?
Name and story	Is your name and story evident across all touchpoints?
Personality and voice	How are you auditing your personality and voice and ensuring consistency across all connection channels?
Visual identity	Does everyone in the company know where to find your brand guidelines and how to utilise them?
Content	Are you analysing your content themes regularly and ensuring they are authentic and encourage connection?

AREA: ELEVATION	
Connection channels	Which reports are you looking at weekly to check the effectiveness of your connection channels?
People	How are you ensuring your staff enjoy where they work, on the daily?
Authority building	How are you working on building your authority each week?
Future thinking	Which analytics show you the impact you're having and is everyone in the company aware of them? How do you share this information?
Analytics and impact	
Alignment	Can you genuinely finish each week feeling in authentic alignment with your brand vision?

What are you doing on the daily?

Are your values front and centre? In my own business, my brand values sit on a post-it note on my computer. As I'm typing this sentence I can see them and I regularly reflect on how I'm showing up for them.

If one of your brand values is 'calm' then how can you cultivate that sense of calm, daily? This may look like lights being dimmed at certain times (without making it unsafe or impairing people's vision), a calming choice of music and never booking meetings without a 15-minute break in between. It may also look like indulging in a one-minute meditation prior to any meetings and/or before anyone starts their work. 'Curiosity' may look like sharing a quick link to something interesting that you have seen or experienced that day. Likewise, 'education' might be discussing something you have just discovered in a 'curiosity' board within a shared content management system.

Planning it out

Let's revisit the At-A-Glance calendar you worked on in Chapter 8 (see Figure 8.3 on page 204) as we look at your brand goals over the next twelve months. (You can also replicate the following process for a three-year or longer-term plan, but using quarters instead of months, i.e. 12 quarters = 3 years.)

First, you want to get REALLY clear on the *brand* objectives you are hoping to achieve in the next twelve months. This could look like increasing brand awareness, growing brand loyalty or celebrating brand values.

Then consider the *business* objectives you are hoping to achieve in the next twelve months. (You may wish to revisit the work you did in Chapter 5 for this.) This could look like an increase in sales, increased retention with staff and stockists or cut-through in a new territory.

Then consider what these objectives actually look like when you break them down into a twelve-month At-A-Glance calendar.

For example, if one of your brand goals is increasing awareness, what are the metrics by which you'll measure its success? Where are you (current state) and where do you want to be (future state) and by when (deadline)?

You might measure this by looking at social media engagement, website traffic, branded search volume, enquiries, sales, referral traffic and links, and social media mentions.

You would then look at your current benchmark for each of these and set a goal for where you'd like each to be, and how much they should increase, by a certain deadline (e.g. 31 December). Mark the deadline into your At-A-Glance calendar.

From there, work back. If you want to hit X number of social mentions between now and 31 December, how many mentions will you need by November? By August? By June? Set monthly targets.

Once you have your monthly targets, you can choose to get granular and set daily targets. Much like if you were working on your health and setting a goal to get in 30 minutes of daily exercise.

Let's say another one of your goals centres around brand loyalty. You may decide that the metrics you'll measure this by will include frequency of purchase, return customers, reviews and testimonials, referral work, and reduced churn on email.

Again, add a future state goal against each metric and a deadline, then input this into your At-A-Glance calendar. Working back, what does this mean per quarter? Per month? Per day?

Seemingly small steps add up. Daily action can lead to magnificent changes over time if you commit to it.

What are you doing on the daily?

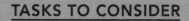

TASKS TO CONSIDER

Daily action adds up and yet it can feel, at times, so hard to figure out. What small action can you take today that will have an impact over time?

Utilising the knowledge you have gained so far, work through the following questions or you can download these in a worksheet form online via the QR code below.

1. *What does showing up to your brand vision look like, on the daily?*

2. *Are your brand values visible to you in some way and how often are you checking the brand activity against them?*

3. *What are your key brand goals over the next twelve months?*

4. *What does this look like for you thirty, sixty and ninety days from now?*

5. *What are your key business goals over the next twelve months?*

6. *Again, what does this look like for you thirty, sixty and ninety days from now?*

7. *How much time can you commit daily to work on these goals?*

Before we jump into Chapter 11, where we look at what happens when things need to change, we'll hear from Abigail Forsyth who, together with her brother Jamie, founded KeepCup after witnessing firsthand the incredible volume of waste with single-use coffee cups.

 Scan for digital worksheet

Business *to* Brand

Photograph by Arsineh Houspian

'The biggest challenges are around people, confidence and timing. Finding the right people, keeping them, but being nimble enough to change direction.'

Profile: *KeepCup*

Almost ten years after opening a cafe together in their hometown of Melbourne, Australia, siblings Abigail and Jamie Forsyth launched KeepCup. Through running the cafe they witnessed a huge volume of waste from single-use coffee cups, the duo did some testing initially with a reusable soup mug and eventually created the globally recognised KeepCup, which has gone on to be used by millions of people worldwide. Here's what co-founder Abigail Forsyth had to say about the brand.

How do you describe KeepCup?

We are on a mission to see a world that neither wants, needs or uses single-use cups.

What do you believe is the difference between running a business and being the custodian of a brand?

An excellent question. They are ultimately the same thing involving a combination of strategic and tactical thinking measured in financial success. Thinking through a brand lens is a way to put the customer and mission first and make decisions that deliver the vision of the business.

How did you have the confidence to come out with KeepCup and did you know, when it started, what a massive impact it would have?

It was less confidence than naive optimism, that people thought and felt as I did that we are trashing the planet to protect destructive cultural norms and business interests. We knew from the outset that the problem was global, and naming the product KeepCup was certainly an 'aha' moment. We were very fortunate that the design resonated with people at a moment when we thought individual behaviour change could get us where we needed to go.

KeepCup has enjoyed global success. What do you think helped?

We followed the interest and let it take us where we found it. The export of Australian and New Zealand light roast [coffee] was also a great benefit to the export of the brand. It's always about connecting with people.

What have been some of the best things you have done to grow the brand over the years?

It all feels a bit wistfully analogue now – exhibiting and sponsoring speciality coffee events, promoting the UGC (user-generated content) we got from Instagram and being really outspoken and single-minded about the issue we are trying to solve.

KeepCup has become such a recognised brand, but it's also become a company that has been copied extensively. How have you managed this both in the business and on a personal level as well?

It's really hard, particularly as the expansion of the 'reuse' category has not solved the problem. We have always had strong IP protection, and unfortunately had to take action a few times with known brands who have breached our IP.

KeepCup has had to defend its association with sustainability – which can be hard as a company grows. It seems whenever a brand gets 'big' it also attracts people who want to pull it down. Which tactics have you employed to deal with this and manage the scrutiny any brand associated with sustainability seems to get?

We have not had any issue around the efficacy of our efforts from B-Corp certification to Life Cycle Analysis and donating 1% of revenue to environmental causes. I did see a placard at a climate march saying 'KeepCup won't save us' – and there certainly has been a bit of a backlash which is understandable. KeepCup is a symbol of individual behaviour change. It has become glaringly obvious that systemic change and legislation is required, so there has been a bit of a sense that KeepCup is a distraction from holding big business and government to account. But, of course, it's not an either/or. The answer is both.

What do you think the biggest myth is around the idea of building a brand today?

That it's new or different.

How has your vision for the company changed over time, or has it remained the same now as it was at the beginning?

The vision remains the same, the means to get there has shifted as the environment around us has changed.

What legacy would you like KeepCup to leave behind?

That we kickstarted the movement from discard to reuse and that we did what we do, and do what we do, with integrity.

What have been some of the biggest challenges you have faced with the brand and how did you work through those?

Gosh there are so many challenges. The biggest challenges are around people, confidence and timing. Finding the right people, keeping them, but being nimble enough to change direction.

When COVID hit we were selling one product that was effectively banned for two years [through the forced closure of cafes and restaurants]. This meant accelerating our product pipeline and dealing with some challenging manufacturing issues.

Most importantly we were a brand that advocates for individual behaviour change and reuse. The pandemic eclipsed these issues, and for a while we really struggled to nuance our brand voice to meet the market. The time it takes for strategies to take shape and brand campaigns to evolve can be destabilising. It takes strength and stamina to maintain confidence and curiosity.

What's the best business advice you have received that you wish you had known when you were starting your brand?

This too shall pass. Although my brother wore that slogan on a T-shirt for almost all of 1998 so I can't say I wasn't told :)

How often do you/the team review the brand and its vision and strategy? How do you do this?

We review the brand daily, weekly, annually. It's a constant conversation. We have probably had a major overhaul of brand and strategy where we have engaged external support every four years. The fundamentals fifteen years on remain. In changes in terms of mission

and values, it's a question of nuancing the way we communicate to find new audiences and meet the changing drivers of individual action and good choices. Unfortunately, the optimism of the early days that individual action could change the world has really come unstuck with the capitalist drivers of GDP, output and convenience – single-use drives the current economic system. It is challenging to encourage people of the value of reuse when new oil and gas fields continue to be opened and native forest logging is still allowed.

In 2020 KeepCup was starting to get pretty shrill, driven by the urgency of what we see needs to happen, but you don't win anyone without a sense of hope, and increasingly a grasp on the absurdity of it all. That's the conversation we are currently having about brand.

Why do you think building a brand, and not simply a business, is important today?

I think they are the same thing, we just think about them differently. Business is thought of in terms of commercials and ownership, brand feels less so because you are thinking from the outside in – what customers value.

Web: keepcup.com

IG: @ keepcup

TT: @keepcup_official

Business *to* Brand

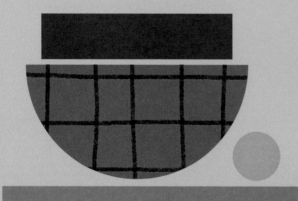

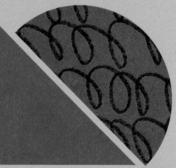
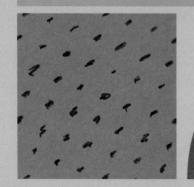

11.

Why change is inevitable

The Ancient Greek philosopher Heraclitus stated, 'There is nothing permanent, except change.' When it comes to your brand, change can often be seen as the enemy. After all, shouldn't you stay consistent and on brand forever?

Not if it no longer works, no longer serves your community and no longer aids in helping the brand achieve its overall vision.

In 2021 I began thinking about changing my own brand, reviewing and tweaking its core message, and looking at how we could go deeper in achieving the initial vision for the company. After months of consideration, research, feedback and internal reviews, a rebrand was confirmed. The brand would change from My Daily Business Coach to My Daily Business. While it may seem ridiculous to simply remove one word from the name, to me and my staff it signalled an expansion. It could now come back to being a brand that is all about how people can love what they do, on the daily. While this may well include coaching, it may just as easily include spending time in nature, connecting with friends, seeing a psychologist or working on their wealth creation with a financial adviser.

Once the decision was made, it was another full year before the rebrand was actualised with a complete revision of the brand guidelines, visual identity, mission statement and objectives. In that time we reviewed our positioning, undertook thorough competitive analysis, and looked at changing up some of our connection channels and content messages.

So when do you know if it's time for a change and how do you know whether you actually need a rebrand or simply a tweak to your existing ACE brand elements?

The answer can be found in your response to the following questions:

1. Is your brand (name, identity, mission, etc.) no longer aligned with your vision for the company?

2. Is your brand failing to serve an audience as you're just unsure of who that audience actually is?

3. Is your brand outdated?

4. Is your brand expanding into categories or areas that feel misaligned with the current brand?

5. Is your brand merging with another company, bringing on a new owner or being acquired by a larger group?

6. Is what you deliver in the brand changing? (This could be your products, services or experiences.)

7. Is your brand experiencing ongoing negative perceptions?

Now, depending on your answers, you may choose to change your messaging, change up your visuals and voice, or tweak your personality and key messages without having to undergo a full rebrand. For others, your answers may signal that a complete overhaul is required. Either way you will need to identify what is not working and why.

In this instance, I like to take on board my ethos of gut and data. You may well have data that can factually show you a decrease in sales, engagement and overall brand loyalty – but it's important to listen to your gut as well.

Why change is inevitable

I always felt a little uncomfortable with the term 'coach' being in my brand name. While I work as a business coach, I have also been called a consultant, mentor, educator and teacher. I didn't want to restrict the brand or myself in years to come by being tied into a name that didn't fully reflect what we were about.

This can be a really confronting space to sit in and I would strongly advise taking the time you need to uncover your answers to the questions above. You don't want to keep changing your brand name, visuals and personality every few months as this will lead to confusion and potentially distrust among your audience.

If you do decide to go forward with a rebrand or change a key part of your brand, look at every one of the ACE brand elements from this new perspective. You may wish to go back through chapters 5, 6 and 7 and ensure you can answer these questions with the new brand in mind.

On a practical level, a change to your brand name, visual identity and tone of voice may mean checking on the following:

1. Online presence

   - domain name
   - backlinks
   - forwarding links
   - social media handles
   - scheduling tools
   - online storage drives and servers (such as Dropbox/Google Drive)
   - inboxes
   - email signatures
   - digital contracts
   - company registration
   - company insurances.

2. Physical presence

   - business cards
   - printed marketing material
   - swing tags and care information
   - packaging
   - branded stationery
   - contracts
   - event collateral
   - uniforms.

You'll also need to be conscious of when and how you launch the rebrand, ensuring that you communicate the change well ahead of time to reduce confusion and potential distrust with your audience. By doing this you're also getting on the front foot and sharing the story and context behind the change rather than having others do this for you.

Change is not easy and changing up your brand is not something you should do on an impulse. And it is possibly harder the longer your business or brand has been established. If you thought getting the internet connected at a new residential home is annoying, try changing your brand name across numerous online tools, platforms, drives and apps.

Yet, sometimes change is necessary in order to grow and fully show up to our overall brand vision. If you do decide to walk this path, I wish you all the best.

(If you want a full version of my own rebrand with all its stressors and challenges including the tediousness of updating online platforms and how to communicate the rebrand, you can check out episode 304 of the *My Daily Business* podcast at mydailybusiness.com/podcast/304.)

> '*Sometimes change is necessary in order to grow and fully show up to our overall brand vision.*'

TASKS TO CONSIDER

Changing your brand or rebranding can be a difficult decision to make. Hopefully the learnings in this chapter will make it easier to take on, if and when you decide to.

Utilising the knowledge you have gained so far, work through the following questions or you can download these in a worksheet form online via the QR code below.

1. *What would you change about your current brand if you could? Why do you think this would be helpful?*

2. *Is there anything about your current brand – name, core messages, vision, audience personas, visual identity – that you feel has to be changed? Why?*

3. *When you consider the future of your brand, is its current positioning working?*

4. *Could you reposition the brand without changing the name, visuals or voice?*

5. *What scares you the most about changing your brand?*

6. *What else would you need to add to the list of digital and physical elements for your particular brand?*

 Scan for digital worksheet

Business *to* Brand

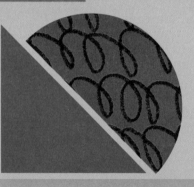
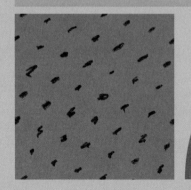

12.

Do you want to build a brand?

Building a brand takes work.

It is not something you can do overnight and it is not something that you accomplish by creating a social media account and slapping a logo on a product. Building a brand, and becoming the custodian for it, is a choice you make every single day and in every action, activity, communication and output of your company.

As we come to the end of this book you may well have decided that as much as you might like to think of your business as a brand, the deep work has not yet been done and perhaps is not something you wish to embark upon. Much like raising a child or being in a long-term committed relationship, creating a brand is something that needs attention, constant self-awareness and a belief that you are contributing to something greater than yourself. It can be an exhausting expedition, with seemingly endless scrutiny of your every action against what you purport to stand for. It can be relentless and thankless, and at times you may wonder why you're bothering at all.

After all, selling something and existing as a purely transactional business is a lot easier in many ways. It doesn't force you to question why you are doing it, the long-term impact it will have on people and the planet, and how its delivery of promise (or failure thereof) can negatively affect everyone from your manufacturers and suppliers through to similar brands who see in your demise the impossibility of their own dreams.

Even with all the hard work and implementation, the path to a brand being successful can sometimes appear a mystery; a puzzle whose last piece seems eternally just out of reach. It can be disheartening when building and maintaining a brand to see a million copycat businesses enter the arena all eager to take your market share, clone your content and seduce your audience.

And yet … So many of us have this longing to create something more meaningful and with a greater legacy than what we imagine a purely transactional business might have. So many of us want to build and cultivate that essence that makes someone feel a deeper connection with what we are creating.

So, what do you want?

There is no right or wrong answer here, only your own response to the question:

Do you want to build a brand?

If the answer is a yes, what sort of brand will it be that you build?

And if the answer is a no, then consider how you may perhaps make a personal impact by supporting other brands and being a part of brand communities that are seeking to invest in a more positive global future.

Not everyone who has a business needs to create a brand.

But if you have reached this part of the book and you're still keen, then I wish you every success as you go about building something meaningful and, in the process, moving people from a simple transaction to an impactful transformation.

Do you want to build a brand?

Tools and resources

Have you ever watched *Ferris Bueller's Day Off*? It was one of my all-time favourite films growing up. One of the best – and most iconic – lines in the film centres on the idea that life moves at a speed that will leave us missing it if we don't become more intentional.

The same can be said for platforms, tools and technology that can help with building your brand. To ensure these tools and resources are still current when you need them, we have created an online resource where you can find a full list of resources and tools, including links that will be updated and changed when necessary.

You can find this at mydailybusiness.com/brandbook.

You can find further information to help you build your brand at:

- mydailybusiness.com/podcast
- mydailybusiness.com/freestuff

For 1:1 business coaching, group coaching or courses, visit mydailybusiness.com/shop

About the author

Fiona Killackey is the founder of My Daily Business (mydailybusiness.com) which helps small business and brand owners (and their teams) understand, create, analyse and improve their brand, marketing, mindset, communications, financials, systems and overall business strategies.

Fiona is a podcaster, award-winning author, speaker, accredited business coach and human trying to navigate life and go to bed feeling like she has done something good that day. With more than two decades of experience working with large and small brands alike (from Amazon and Country Road Group, through to CULTIVER and Collective Closets), Fiona understands what it takes to create a business that is financially secure and emotionally fulfilling.

Fiona was raised by incredible parents who promoted education and kindness as two of the most important facets of life. It's these beliefs that fuel My Daily Business – which offers free education via a popular twice-weekly podcast, weekly Sunday email and Instagram and TikTok posts, as well as affordable courses, DIY business templates, Sidestep the Hustle group coaching programs and a range of 1:1 business coaching packages.

Fiona lives in North Warrandyte with her husband and their two children and two dogs.

You can connect with Fiona at:

Web: mydailybusiness.com

E: hello@mydailybusiness.com

IG: @mydailybusiness_

TT: @mydailybusiness

Image: Hilary Walker Photography (hilarywalker.com.au)

Business *to* Brand

Acknowledgements

I have to start with a BIG thank you to the readers of *Passion. Purpose. Profit.* – my first book. Since it was published in September 2020, when the whole world seemed to be in an incredibly uncertain state, I have been the recipient of so many messages, emails and DMs from people all over the world; Tuscany to Toronto, New Jersey to New Caledonia. Whenever I doubted myself in writing this book, when I let my insecurities get the better of me, it was your messages, your notes and your enthusiasm for the first book that kept me going. Thank you to every single person who read, shared, promoted, stocked, recommended and sold that first book. I am hoping this second book makes you just as excited to keep reading.

To my volunteer focus group who kindly gave their time and insights into the making of this, thank you – James Young, Rocios Vazquez and Renee White. Thank you to Anne-Claire Petre for checking my French!

To my amazing Hardie Grant team, thank you. While it's the author's name on any book, behind them is an entire team of cheerleaders, supporters and people so skilled in their craft. A massive thank you to Alice Hardie-Grant, Tahlia Anderson, Elena Callcott, Camha Pham, Hannah Schubert, Kristin Thomas, Andrea O'Connor and Roxy Ryan. Thank you also Andy Warren for coming on board again as the designer for this book and bringing this all to life visually so we can continue to fight the war against boring business book designs!

A big thank you to those brand founders and company MDs/CDs who generously gave their insights for this book – Becca Stern, Laura Thompson, Abigail Forsyth, Sandra Velasquez, Mark Adams, Petah Marian and Arjen Klinkenberg.

To date I have worked with hundreds of small business owners in 1:1 coaching sessions and thousands more across masterclasses, workshops, group coaching programs and my online courses. It is such a privilege to ride the journey of small business with you, see the world through your lens and learn from you all. So many of you encouraged me with this second book, shared your stories and helped me gain the confidence to put this out. Thank you for trusting me with your brands and your dreams – it is so very appreciated.

Thank you to Melia Rayner, Jenny Nyugen and Chriss Mannix for your guidance in getting this book out into the world.

To those close to me who have listened patiently as I workshopped ideas for this book, relayed my challenges and celebrated the small wins, thank you. In particular Faustina Agolley, Paul Darragh, Phoebe Bell, Marre Smit, Cecil and Helen Killacky, Sinéad de Gooyer, Andrea Telford and Sarah Kwan.

Thank you to Ma. Yricka Juje T Navarro for constantly smiling while playing yet another game of Tetris with my schedule so this book could get written. Your enthusiasm and encouragement is deeply appreciated.

To Dr Eric Maisel, thank you for reminding me that the mystery in life is just as important as the results. And to Simran Kaur for empowering an entire generation of women to educate themselves around what they really want from life – and for agreeing to be one of the first readers of this book.

To Mum and Dad, thank you for instilling in me an inner strength to keep going when life gets hard, and to always believe in the good in humanity. These last few years have been some of the hardest for myself and for so many small business owners trying to create brands that matter. It is your influence that has allowed me to get up, keep going and share that determination with others. Thank you for being 'parents first' and my greatest teachers in life. I miss you both every single day.

To my beautiful boys, Levi and Elio, who remind me every day why I do what I do and how important the seemingly ordinary, everyday moments are. It is your generation that I hope benefits most from the people behind brands rethinking how and what and why they do what they do, and putting more of a focus on people and the planet, rather than profit.

Finally, to my husband, Jerome Rebeiro, to whom I regularly lay out my fears, hopes, dreams, insecurities and wins, and who gently takes each into consideration before reminding me what's most important and of who I really am. I could not have written this book without your love, encouragement, humour and support. Gang160 for life.

Business *to* Brand

Notes

Notes

Notes

Notes

Published in 2024 by Hardie Grant Books, an imprint of Hardie Grant Publishing

Hardie Grant Books (Melbourne)
Wurundjeri Country
Building 1, 658 Church Street
Richmond, Victoria 3121

Hardie Grant North America
2912 Telegraph Ave
Berkeley, California 94705

hardiegrant.com/books

Hardie Grant acknowledges the Traditional Owners of the Country on which
we work, the Wurundjeri People of the Kulin Nation and the Gadigal People
of the Eora Nation, and recognises their continuing connection to the land,
waters and culture. We pay our respects to their Elders past and present.

 A catalogue record for this
book is available from the
National Library of Australia

Business to Brand
ISBN 978 1 74379 971 0
ISBN 978 1 76144 137 0 (ebook)

10 9 8 7 6 5 4 3 2 1

Publisher: Alice Hardie-Grant, Tahlia Anderson
Project Editor: Elena Callcott
Editor: Camha Pham
Design Manager: Kristin Thomas
Designer: Andy Warren
Head of Production: Todd Rechner
Production Controller: Jessica Harvie

Colour reproduction by Splitting Image Colour Studio

 Printed in China by Leo Paper Products LTD.

The paper this book is printed on is from
FSC®-certified forests and other sources.
FSC® promotes environmentally responsible,
socially beneficial and economically viable
management of the world's forests.

FSC
www.fsc.org
MIX
Paper | Supporting
responsible forestry
FSC® C020056